RECAP

"An Applicable Overview of Biblical Principles"

COLUMBUS CODY III

Copyright 2016 by Columbus Cody III.
Printed in the United States of America
ISBN: 978-0-9975473-1-3

Connect with the author:
Twitter: **@ccody3**
Email: *got2liveright@gmail.com*

CONTENTS

INTRODUCTION

Do you like drama, murder mystery, thrillers, horror, the Supernatural, or even romance? What if I were to tell you that you could find all of these and much more within the pages of the Holy Bible? The purpose of Recap is to encourage my readers to give the Bible a chance! In the pages that follow, you will be provided with an overview of 14 common and very important principles found in the Bible.

Many people say that the Bible is boring or too hard to read and understand. I used to be one of those people until the words of God came alive for me! Now, I love what I learn in the pages of the Bible and I want everyone to experience that same excitement. I can still remember the exact moment and the exact passage that I was reading in the Bible when the Bible just seemed to "make sense" to me. I awoke early on a Saturday morning with a desire to spend some time with God. There is no greater feeling that waking up with God centered in your heart and thoughts of Him flooding your mind. On that morning I was reading verses in the Gospel of John. I cannot remember exactly how many chapters I read that day but when I got to John 16:33 it was as if the whole world just paused for a moment. All went silent. I read the words of that verse, and then I read them again. A smile started to form on my face, and then I couldn't help but to say, "Thank you, Lord!" I could tell you what is written in that verse but maybe leaving you wondering what that verse has to say will add enough suspense to get you to open up your Bible at this very moment. In fact, let's all put down this book just for a moment and look up John 16:33. It's in the New Testament. Matthew, Mark, Luke, and John! You found it, you've reached your destination. Now flip your page or scroll your screen if you're searching on a tablet or your phone to chapter 16. Get ready! Are you getting excited yet? Look at verse 33. Read it out loud to yourself. Did you feel that? I love this verse because now I know without any doubt that I, too, am an overcomer because Jesus is my Lord and He overcame the world. Okay, now you can pick up this book again and let's continue on our journey.

Not too long ago, I developed a lesson for one of our Wednesday night Bible study classes at my church. I've been told by quite a few people and I've finally come to believe and appreciate that God has given me a gift for teaching and making things understandable but exciting at the same time. After seeing that the lesson, that I titled *A Recap of the Word of God*, had an impact on the group that night I knew that more needed to be said. While I was driving into work a few days after that Wednesday night class, I heard what I believe was God speaking into my spirit. I could hear loudly and clearly that the lesson that I taught the few people in that small group setting that evening needed to be shared with the world. What you will read in the coming pages is my attempt to share information from that evening's lesson as well as many other lessons that God has shown me since.

RECAP

Recap is by no means exhaustive, but as you read it, I pray that you will be able to see the 'big picture' of what the Bible is about. It is my hope that after reading the pages that follow, you will develop an appetite for and an intense appreciation for the greatest book ever written- the Holy Bible.

CHAPTER 1

REBELLION

rebellion: refusal to obey rules or accept normal standards of behavior
Merriam-Webster Dictionary

In the beginning God created a beautiful and wonderful world. There was no need. There was no lack. There was nothing but peace and tranquility. So what happened? What changed? What made everything go wrong? One word: Rebellion.

God created everything that the eye can see but His greatest creation, His soon to be most difficult creation, was the man. When He made man there was harmony between God and man. There was peace and fellowship between the infinite and the finite. There was nothing that could come between them. Or was there? It is easy for us to judge our forefather Adam and say if we had that same type of relationship with God we would NEVER mess that up. The irony is this: Christ died to grant us the ability to have that same type of closeness to God, and yet we still find ourselves refusing to obey His rules and refusing to accept His standard of living. We too are rebellious.

When God formed the soil and handmade his greatest creation – the man – He was very pleased with what He had done. In fact, Genesis tells us that God said that His creations were very good. He made us in His image. Not that we "look like" God physically, but that we have within us the same structure as God. When He created man, He gave the man what we call a free will. This means that mankind has the ability and privilege to make our own decisions. Ultimately, He desires that we choose Him and His ways, but He allows us to make that choice. God cannot and would not be glorified if He had to force His will upon us. The glory comes when we are presented with "opportunities" from the world and also presented with the truth of God's Word, and we choose God and His word over our flesh's desires.

When God placed Adam and Eve in the garden and gave them EVERYTHING that their hearts desired, He also gave them one rule. One rule! No long laundry list of things that He needed done by the end of the day. There were no deadlines thrust upon their shoulders. There was no pressure to perform. One rule! And that one rule was, "Hey Adam, listen I'm gonna let you have anything and everything in the garden for your enjoyment, but I need to you to do one thing for me. Stay away from this tree over here. This tree is called the Tree of Knowledge of Good and Evil. This tree I don't want you to eat from. In fact, don't even touch this tree. You understand?"

When God commands us to stay away from something, He is not trying to keep us away from something good. He is only trying to help us avoid something that will bring harm or separation to the relationship that we have with Him. When we choose in favor of what we think we want over what God wants in our lives, it is called rebellion. Rebellion always leads to separation. Rebellion never shows itself as a negative. Rebellion presents itself as a pleasure or a promising opportunity. Rebellion won't shout loudly that it will lead us away from God and ultimately to our death. Rebellion will slyly say just as the serpent in the Garden of Eden did, "You won't surely die."

"I know what the Bible says, but…" These are some dangerous words to speak. But these are words we hear often and may have even spoken frequently ourselves. We don't want to consider ourselves as rebels. We don't like to admit that we sometimes totally disregard God's command over our lives. We sometimes try to justify our faulty decisions and rebellious motives by saying that God understands that we will make mistakes. While God does understand all things, it doesn't mean God accepts all things.

Rebellion has a way of leading us further away from God than we could ever think or imagine. Picture this: you live in Heaven, and on a daily basis you get to see the road paved in gold, the crystal stream, the tree of life, and the majestic angelic beings. You get to hear the beautiful songs of the heavenly hosts. You observe the angels bowing before God saying Holy, Holy, Holy every time they come up and see His glory. You, yourself, are given the opportunity to stand in the very presence of God at all times. Who would mess that up? Who would object to that? Well, there was one named Lucifer who decided he'd rather be in God's position than serve in the position that God created for him. He decided to rebel against the one and only God. The Almighty God! Rebellion has a way of leading us farther away from God than we thought it would. There is an old English proverb that says, "When the sword of rebellion is drawn, the sheath should be thrown away."

I am certain that Lucifer – a.k.a. Satan, a.k.a the Devil – never thought that his rebellion would lead to his demise. Believe it or not, Satan's greatest trick is to disguise our acts of rebellion, blinding us of the consequences of our rebellious acts. In Genesis, when he deceived Eve in the Garden of Eden, he downplayed the fact that her actions would be considered rebellious. He presented the choice as something to be desired above all other things. He made it seem as if she was being deprived of something from God. Psalm 84:11 says "No good thing will He withhold from them that walk uprightly." God only desires to keep things away from His children that would harm them. Eve, not seeing her choice as rebellion, chose her desire over God's command but we must not be fooled. We must understand and acknowledge that whenever we choose what we want over what God commands it is called REBELLION!

Once Eve rebelled against God's instructions, she came to her husband Adam, and he joined her in the rebellion. And then: Boom! The entire world changed. Rebellion always leads to a change. The cherished relationship that they once shared with God and with nature changed. The way they saw the world changed. The fate of all mankind changed – all because of the rebellious act of one man and one woman. We should never think that our acts of rebellion against God will affect only us. Every man or woman born after the creation of Adam and Eve has dealt with the pressures and problems of life that were brought on by that one decision made in the garden to disobey God.

The decision to rebel against God's command by Adam and Eve became a decision that has shaped and molded mankind's thought process ever since. Psalm 51:5 tells us that we are born and shaped in iniquity and with sinful natures. We were born with a natural pull toward rebellion. It is much easier to do the wrong thing than to do the right thing. Our initial impulses are to pull against, to look for the loopholes, and to find ways to cut corners. This is not something that many of us take notice of because often times we view these actions as the norm.

I have two sons. At the time that I'm writing this book they are 4 years old and 2 years old. I've never taught my sons to say the word NO but they learned that dreaded word nonetheless. My youngest son answers nearly every question with a quick NO. I could ask him if he wants candy and he'd say NO. Of course, being 2 years old, he is still learning to talk and this is an innocent mistake, but the fact that NO is his response speaks clearly of mankind's natural inclination to rebel, to say no, or to disobey. The rebellion of one affected the destiny of all.

Nothing good comes from rebelling against God. The Bible says in 2 Corinthians 6:14, "Be ye not unequally yoked together with unbelievers: for what fellowship hath righteousness with unrighteousness? And what communion hath light with darkness?" In the past we've interpreted this verse to mean that Christians shouldn't marry people who are unbelievers or non-Christians. Rebelling against this command of God has landed many in the divorce courts. God wants His people to have wonderful and full lives, but whenever we choose to rebel against God we open ourselves up to things He wanted to shield us from, and we end up closing ourselves off from His blessings. God doesn't have a desire to micromanage our lives and pick and choose every single thing we do. What He does want is to help us avoid unneeded distractions, problems, and pains. He wants to provide us with the abundant and blessed life that Christ died to make available.

There are various passages found throughout the Bible that expose God's feelings toward fornication. He isn't trying to keep us from fun. He's trying to keep us from destruction. With the decision to rebel and engage in fornication come the possibilities of many devastating things; disease, unwanted pregnancies, baby mama drama, abandoned children, child neglect and abuse, and the list can go on and on. God never intended for us to endure these problems but when we choose to rebel the consequences are set in motion.

There was once a great king and he had accomplished great things. He had defeated many foes. He was considered by many to be a great success. One day he decided he wanted to see just what he had accomplished. He wanted to count up all that "he had done". He wanted to count and see how many men he had in his army. He wanted to see what type of arsenal he had to fight with. No harm in double checking to see how many fighting men you have, right? I mean what great leader doesn't know exactly what weapons he has at his disposal? The problem in this situation is this, God instructed King David not to count the men. He didn't want David to count on men, but to continue to place his trust in God. This story can be found in 1Chronicles 21:1-14. Pride is one of man's worst enemies. Pride always leads to a fall and it always leads to destruction. King David's pride caused him to make a move that may seem small or insignificant to us, but was considered disobedience and ultimately a great rebellion against God. Because of this decision, God sent word to this great king. God told David that he had to choose his own punishment. He could choose three years of famine or three months of warring with his enemies, or 3 days of dealing with plagues in the lands.

One of the most powerful lessons I've learned in my Christian journey is that God is really good at teaching His children a lesson. He is the master disciplinarian. He knows how to drive home a point so that His children think twice before engaging in the wrong behavior again. This reminds me of when I was young and we were disobedient; my mother would give us the option of taking a spanking or dealing with punishment. It always felt like a lose-lose situation. The spanking would only last a short while compared to the punishment, but the pain of the spanking would be more intense than that of the punishment. Because I always hated getting a spanking, I often decided to choose the punishment. I remember one time in particular that it felt like those few days of punishment took years to pass. Mom's point was forever etched into my mind. I don't like spankings, and God forbid I would have to stay in the house when all of the fun things were going on outside. It was time to make a change. I needed to change my attitude, I needed to change my behavior, and I needed to change my mindset to one that sought to please my mother rather than to please myself. This is God's desire for us as well. I am sure God doesn't take pleasure in disciplining His children, but because He loves us, He will make sure we learn our lessons. Sometimes when we have a "hard head" or when we have a rebellious spirit, it means we will have to learn things "the hard way". It would be far better for us to develop self-discipline than to force God to exercise His righteous discipline.

One thing that I am eternally grateful for is that even though we have rebelled against God, He has not dealt with us according to our rebellion. God still sees there is good within us and gives us time to discover, embrace, and live according to that good. We may even find that we've behaved and lived our lives similar to how the Children of Israel (God's chosen people) lived in the Bible. It was a constant cycle of rebellion: asking God for forgiveness and help, being rescued by God, and then rebelling again. When we choose to live rebellious lives we will slow down the progress and promises that God wants to see happen in our lives. It took the Israelites 40 years to cover the distance that should have taken only a couple days because of the constant disobedience and rebellion. Can you image walking around in circles for 40 years because you would not follow directions, because you were rebellious? I've heard women joke about their husbands and say that they won't seek directions and so they will remain lost and drive around in circles because they refuse to ask for guidance. Most of the people of Israel died while in the wilderness. Rebelling against God could be a very costly decision, and if we don't act quickly it could become a deadly decision. Just ask the Israelites.

REFLECT AND CONNECT

1. Think about a time where you felt led by the Spirit but you chose to go the opposite way. What bad things came about from that choice?
2. If you could go back and make sure you didn't rebel against God in one specific situation in your life, what would that be?
3. What steps will you take now to help you rebel less and obey more?

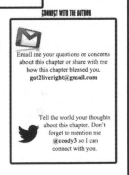

CONNECT WITH THE AUTHOR

Email me your questions or concerns about this chapter or share with me how this chapter blessed you.
got2liveright@gmail.com

Tell the world your thoughts about this chapter. Don't forget to mention me @ccody3 so I can connect with you.

CHAPTER 2

REDEMPTION

redemption: deliverance upon payment of ransom; rescue
thefreedictionary.com

Because of the choice that Adam made many years ago, we have all been born with a destiny of death. All humans who has been born since that act of rebellion took place in the Garden of Eden no longer have to accept this destiny if they do not want to. The reason that we no longer have to accept our much deserved death sentence has nothing to do with what we've done or what we can do but everything to do with what Jesus Christ did for us on Calvary. Redeeming mankind was not an easy task nor did it come at an inexpensive cost. It cost Jesus his life and every ounce of blood that flowed through his body. He gave up his life so that he could redeem us and bring us back to God. Every day we should find ourselves verbally thanking Christ for paying this enormous price and for rescuing us from that awful destiny. And after we verbalize it, after we say it with our lips, we must then live it. We begin to live a life of gratitude.

I think many of us are glad that Jesus died for our sins, but I don't think many of us fully grasp what that truly means. I like to think of it like this. Picture an old courtroom. The wooden desks and seats are perfectly aligned and their flawless shine is evidence that the cleaning crew never misses a spot. You are sitting at the table labeled Defendant but there is no one sitting beside you. There is no defense attorney, no counselor, no one. You are on your own. As you sit there you hear the thunderous voice of the prosecution go on and on about what you've done wrong and calling out all of your sins one by one. The funny thing is, everything that you are being accused of is true. There is no disputing it. You did it, and you're guilty of every charge! The judge sits up high in his seat. You struggle to look in his direction because there is something about him that makes you feel dirty. Your guilt won't allow you to hold eye contact longer than a second or two. Nothing seems to get past him. He listens intently to all of the charges brought against you. He clears his throat and sadly looks down to where you sit. "Will the defendant please rise!" he says with a hint of pain in his voice. It doesn't appear that he is going to enjoy the news that he is about to deliver.

"Because of the evidence that has been presented against you, I have no choice but to sentence you to the maximum allowable sentence. Because of your transgressions and the lifestyle you've decided to live, I am sentencing you to the death penalty." You sit there dumbfounded, trying to come up with the words to save yourself. Nothing comes to the surface. You know that you are getting what you deserve, but you wish there were some way to get out of it. You wish that someone would come and rescue you.

Sitting on death row is the worst. Life seems to just run around in circles as you await that dreaded day. You know it's coming, but you try to distract yourself from that truth. You go through the motions of everyday life and try to keep yourself busy with anything and everything that seems entertaining enough to keep your mind off of the truth of your destiny. You keep hearing others talking about some lawyer or counselor who has been getting people released. You chalk it up as a "too good to be true" story and so you don't pay it any mind. After all, you truly did everything that landed you in this place. You deserve to be here. No one put you here but yourself. You chose to do the things you did, to say the things you said, to act the way you did. The more time you sit and think the more you find yourself questioning why you are the way you are. What made you act this way? What makes you desire the things you do? Why did you choose this path when it is obviously wrong?

One morning you wake up and start your day in your cell the same way you've done since you arrived. You walk over to your rusty sink to turn on the hot water but the water never seems to get warmer than room temperature. You grab your face towel that hangs on the screw sticking out of the wall. You knock the cockroach that crawls on your towel to the floor and step on it. It makes a crunching sound loud enough to wake up the other inmates. It's a shame that this has become the norm of your life. You think to yourself: Why would anyone want to live like this? You hear footsteps coming down the corridor but you don't think much of it, this too is normal on the Row. The footsteps are getting closer and then they stop. You take the face towel down from your face as a voice startles you.

"Hey, word just came down! Tomorrow is your big day, Buddy."

"What big day?" you snap back.

"Tomorrow is when you meet your maker." The deputy says with a smirk on his face, as you catch the tone of satisfaction in his voice.

You slowly sit back down on your bunk. You wait for the guard to move further down the hall and you break down. The tears seem to fall for hours. Your head begins to throb from all of the crying. Suddenly you feel this awkward feeling in your chest. Is this a heart attack? Your heart really hurts. For the first time you feel bad about not living right. You slide down to your knees from the bunk. It is hard for any words to escape your lips.

"Oh God, I'm sorry. I'm sorry. I'm so sorry." Now these few words continue to flow from your lips as the tears continue to flood your face. Images start flashing through your memory. You see yourself as a little boy going to church with your grandmother. It seems like every pleading word that she spoke comes rushing at you at once.

"Give your life to God, Baby. He will always be there for you. No matter what you've done wrong or how far out there in the world you get, He will welcome you back." Her words seem to pierce your heart and the sobbing continues. You regret not honoring the words that she poured out over you. You remember the time that you walked past her room and overheard her praying for you. You remember the sadness in her voice, the pain as each word escaped her lips. You remember what she told you before she breathed her last breath. "Give your life to God, Baby."

You lie in the bunk squeezing your pillow. The second hand on the clock sounds like a drum in your ear. The seconds that had been moving so slowly before seem to rush now. You wish you could reach up and grab the clock and push the time back. Push it all the way back. Back to a time before you did the things you did. Back to a time before you were so rebellious. But it's too late now, or is it?

You hear this gentle and quiet voice whispering in your ear. "Pray about it. Tell God that you need His help." You think to yourself how it wouldn't make a difference now. You say to yourself that you should have done that years ago. It's too late for me, you think. That opportunity has passed you by and now you are a hopeless case. You hear the voice again, speaking the same instructions but this time the words are louder and more stern. You begin trying to remember how your grandmother taught you to pray. If you're going to be punished for your rebellious and sinful choices tomorrow, it couldn't hurt to say a prayer.

"Lord," your voice shakes as you try to put together words you feel God might listen to. "I know it's been a long time since I've called on you. I've lived a horrible life. I've done things that were bad and I've broken probably every commandment that you have. I don't even know if you are hearing this prayer right now but I want you to know that I'm sorry. I'm not just saying this because of what is going to happen to me; I really am sorry. I wish I could go back and have another chance to live a better life. Please help me. Amen."

You lie in your bed all night thinking about what will happen to you in the coming hours. You start remembering all of the stories you've heard about what happens when you die. The tears begin to build up in your eyes again. Your heart starts to race and you get a weird taste in your mouth. You jump to your feet to run to the toilet. You feel as though you're going to be sick. The words that the guard said earlier keep playing in your mind like a scratched CD stuck on the same track. "Meet your maker, meet your maker, meet your maker." You remember the slight grin on his face, and you think: How could someone take pleasure in another person's pain?

You doze off but quickly wake up again. Who could sleep in a situation like this? This goes on all night. You are exhausted. You are tired of worrying and tired of wondering. And then your hear it. Those same footsteps you heard yesterday. Each one getting louder and closer. Your heart rate elevates with each step. Outside of your cell stand several men. One is holding what appears to be a Bible in his hand. His voice has a kind ring to it. "Would you like me to pray with you?" He asks.

"Yes, I would like that very much!" The words anxiously fly from your lips.

"Do you believe that God can save you and that He wants to save you? Do you believe that Jesus Christ is the son of God? Do you want to go to heaven?" His questions seem so heavy and so hard to handle. But you listen and respond with boldness and courage.

"Yes, I believe! Yes, I want to be saved! Yes, I want to go to heaven!"

"It's time," one of the guards behind you says, bringing you back to reality. For a moment, life was sweet. For a moment you forgot about what lay ahead. As you sit on the bunk, one of the guards kneels down and puts the ice cold shackles around your ankles and then he slowly helps you to your feet. The other guard hands him another set of restraints.

"Put your hands out in front of you, please." He takes the restraints and places them around each of your hands and locks them into place. The restraints minimize your movement greatly. Now you have to shuffle in order to walk. The two guards stand on either side of you. Both of them grab your arms to help you shuffle down the hall. They both move in a very orderly and precise manner, almost robotic.

You say to yourself, "I wonder how many times these guys have done this."

The door to the chamber is getting closer and closer. Your shuffled steps are getting shorter and shorter. If it weren't for the guards, your steps probably would have stopped, but their grasps seem to continue to guide you toward the door. Your heart is pounding. Your breathing becomes shallow. Sweat begins pouring down your forehead as they bring you into this room of death. It is cleaner than you imagined it would be and the smell of the room seems out of place as well. The guards lower you into an old leathery seat and connect more straps to the restraints that are already around your ankles and wrists.

The numbers on the clock on the wall above your head switch from 8:59 to 9:00. "We are ready." The guard says as he pushes an intercom button to speak to someone outside the room.

"Alright, everyone out of the room please," the voice on the intercom responds. Everyone in the room start filing out one by one. You start to pray again, silently.

"Lord, please forgive me. I really am sorry for what I've done. Please make room for me in heaven. I'm scared, Jesus."

As you are praying you overhear several men speaking over the intercom. It appears that they forgot to push the button to turn it off. You can hear everything.

"Let him go." These words come from a voice that you haven't heard before. You listen and try to figure out who might be trying to help get you out of this situation.

"We can't just let him go; this man has been sentenced to die!"

"Let him go." The voice repeats. It is a soft and gentle voice, yet powerful at the same time.

"This is the punishment that he deserves! You heard all the things that he did. Death is what he deserves."

"Fine, if death is what is needed to make things right, let me take his place."

17

Everyone gets quiet. No one knows what to say or what to do. The guards look at one another confused and amazed.

"Wait a minute! You mean to tell me that you are willing to die for this man? After hearing about what kind of person he is? You are willing to trade places and die for something that you didn't do? Why?"

"Because I love him. Now let him go."

REFLECT AND CONNECT

1. How does understanding the gift of redemption affect how you live your life?
2. How would you explain to another person that you KNOW that you've been redeemed?
3. Make a list of the wrong things that you've done that you don't want anyone to know about. If you've asked Jesus to save you and to rule your heart and to be your Lord, take a pen and scratch each one out one at a time and say, "Thank you, Lord" after each one.

CONNECT WITH THE AUTHOR

Email me your questions or concerns about this chapter or share with me how this chapter blessed you.
got2liveright@gmail.com

Tell the world your thoughts about this chapter. Don't forget to mention me @ccody3 so I can connect with you.

CHAPTER 3

REPENTANCE

repentance: to feel remorse, contrition, or self-reproach for what one has done or failed to do
thefreedictionary.com

W e've all done wrong. We were born with an inclination to do wrong. To lie, steal, and cheat is the common ground of the human condition. Rebellion against God led us down a road that would require redemption. Jesus provided that redemption but now we must repent. I've never really cared much for the "dictionary" definition of repentance. It has never left me feeling satisfied with an understanding of what it truly means to repent. But one day I heard my pastor preach a sermon that made this one word come alive in my spirit. To repent is not just about feeling bad or remorseful for what we've done or haven't done. To repent is to do something about that feeling I'm having. To truly repent means to change! To truly repent means to turn from my way of doing things and to turn toward God's ways of doing things.

Several years ago I released a podcast titled *The 3 little C's and the Big Big R*. It was based on a message I had heard in our church many times. The three little C's were conviction, confession, and contrition and the Big Big R was repentance. I believe that many people are confused about repentance- just as I once was. Repentance is not conviction. Repentance is not confession. Repentance is not contrition. Experiencing and embracing these three little C's is very important for all believers, but if we never get to the point of repentance, then these three little C's really don't matter. If we are going to live a life that is pleasing to God, we must repent. We must change. We must turn back to God and turn away from sin.

CONVICTION

Conviction is a good thing! That is the feeling you get deep down in your gut that you are wrong. It is an awareness that the behaviors that you are engaged in are not of God and do not please God. When you experience conviction it means that God is attempting to speak to you about where you are in life. It means that the Holy Spirit has not given up on you. It means that God still sees value in you and wants to redirect you back to him. If you cannot feel the guilt of your wrongdoing and you cannot muster any remorse for your wrongdoings, then you are in a sad place. Many people don't think God would want His people to feel guilty, but if we never felt the impact of our misdeeds and if we had no awareness that we were off base with the Lord, we'd never get back on track. If we are ever going to get to a point where we will change, we are going to first have to be aware that change is needed.

Some call it our conscience, but believers call it the Holy Spirit. That quiet voice you hear that instructs, guides, and corrects. When you are about to say something that you know you shouldn't, you hear the voice speak. "Don't say that! God wouldn't be glorified if you say that. Your testimony and your ability to be an effective witness may be compromised if you say that." You hear the voice, but you still have to make the choice. What will you do? Will you honor the voice or will you give in to your flesh? Will you do what makes you happy or what makes God happy? When we give in and do what our flesh desires, many times after the fact we will feel a sense of loss. We will feel a sense of regret and of guilt. Everyone experiences choosing what they want over and against what God wants, but some people don't feel the sting of conviction. This is unfortunate, because that sting is what is needed to lead us to repentance.

CONFESSION

Confession is not repentance. Conviction brought about the awareness that we were wrong, whereas a confession takes place when we admit that we are wrong. Confessing our sins is vital to establishing and maintaining a relationship with the Lord. Admitting that we are wrong is one of the first steps to living a successful Christian life. But it cannot stop there. Admitting that we are wrong means nothing if we have no desire to change, to repent. Whenever you see the AA meetings in the movies or television shows, the speakers always starts out by saying their names and then confessing that they are alcoholic. Admitting this fact is one of the first steps of their recovery. No changes can be made until you first admit that a change needs to be made.

One of the problems that many of us have with confession is that it forces us to truly look at ourselves. All of our flaws and weaknesses are brought before us. Sometimes it can be scary and downright ugly. But if we do not confess and admit that we are wrong and unworthy, we will never appreciate the redemptive act that Jesus performed at Calvary, and ultimately we will not repent. I believe that the reason so many of us take for granted or aren't overjoyed and overwhelmed by what Jesus did for us is that many of us won't really admit how awful we once were.

Another problem is that some think that they have repented when they've only confessed. This is one of the great tricks and schemes of the Devil. He doesn't mind us admitting our wrongs, but he will fight the believer with all that he has to make sure we never turn away from our wrongs. People attend church Sunday after Sunday and confess, saying things like, "I know I'm wrong…" It is very dangerous to think that we've repented when all that we've done is admitted that we were wrong. What do we do after we acknowledge our wrong? Admitting we're wrong doesn't make things right. Admitting our sins doesn't cover our sins. Admitting we are wrong doesn't mean a thing if we aren't going to change that which is wrong.

CONTRITION

Contrition is much more than feeling bad about disappointing God. It's more like your heart is broken because you've broken God's (your Father's) heart. It is a deep sorrow that you feel because you have again shamed God and not upheld the promise you made to live for Him. King David was known as a "man after God's own heart" because when he did mess up (which he did more often than we may realize) he was deeply sorrowful and moved to get right with God. Contrition plays an important role in the process of returning to right standing with God; but again, we cannot confuse contrition with repentance. Just because we feel sorry about what we've done and we feel deep regret and sorrow that we've let God down and not upheld our end of the relationship, it means nothing if that sorrow doesn't move us to change. If the sorrow doesn't lead us to abstaining from sin, then all we've really experienced is a shift in our emotions and not a shift of our lifestyle.

In 2 Chronicles 7:14, God doesn't move until after His people "turn" from their wicked ways. To turn is to repent. To turn means to change. In the passage, God doesn't move after they humble themselves or when they pray or even when they seek His face. He moves on behalf of the people after they turn from their wicked ways. God only hears from heaven and heals their land AFTER the people realize they are wrong (conviction), admit that they are wrong (confession), experience deep sorrow for their unrighteous living (contrition) and then TURN from their wicked ways (repentance).

REFLECT AND CONNECT

1. Why do you think many find it easy to confess but not to repent?
2. What sins have you found yourself repeating but you know you must turn away from?
3. After repenting, what do you think you must do in order to guard your heart from returning to the sin?

CONNECT WITH THE AUTHOR

Email me your questions or concerns about this chapter or share with me how this chapter blessed you.
got2liveright@gmail.com

Tell the world your thoughts about this chapter. Don't forget to mention me @ccody3 so I can connect with you.

CHAPTER 4

REBORN

Jesus answered and said unto him, Verily, verily, I say unto thee, except a man be born again, he cannot see the kingdom of God.
John 3:3 KJV

What does it mean to be a "born again" believer? I remember the first time I heard someone ask me if I was saved and if I had been born again. It was terms that seemed so simple to define and understand but I had no idea of what they meant exactly. I answered like I think most people do. I explained how I was born and raised in the church, but that doesn't really answer the question. Many people faithfully attend church their entire lives, yet many of these same people have never truly experienced God's saving power. Many of them have never been born again.

If we are still living according to the "old man's" ideas and philosophies, then we have not come to know God because to know God is to love God, and loving God leads us to live a certain way. An easy argument that can be made is that anyone who says that he/she is a believer and has been born again, yet still lives a lifestyle deeply rooted in sinful behavior, expressing no desire to give that lifestyle up, is not a child of God and has not been reborn. The Bible makes it very clear that many of us are deceiving ourselves when we think that we have been reborn when there aren't any changes coming forth from our lives. Change is the truest sign for us and all those that know us that we truly have been born again.

Being born again is something that a believer should proudly profess. We should enthusiastically express this through our everyday behaviors (how we talk, how we treat others, as well as what we engage in and what we avoid). Being born again isn't something we should struggle to explain to someone when they ask us why we do what we do or why we behave in the manner that we do. In 1 Peter 3:15b, Peter explains to born again believers that we shouldn't shy away from being a mouthpiece for the Lord. We should love explaining to others what it means to be reborn. "And be ready always to give an answer to every man that asketh you a reason of the hope that is in you with meekness and fear."

Every time I think about how my destiny has changed from spending eternity in Hell to having a mansion in Heaven and from eternal damnation to eternal fellowship and communion with God, I get excited about being redeemed and reborn. A truth that we must never forget is that when we were born we were born WRONG. In Psalm 51:5 David wrote, "Behold, I was shapen in iniquity; and in sin did my mother conceive me." So since we were born wrong, the only remedy is to be born again. We must be reborn if we want to be with God. Thank God that we don't have to be a perfect man or woman to come to Jesus. But we cannot remain the same and expect to enter the kingdom of God. In the third chapter of John's Gospel, Jesus explains to a man named Nicodemus that he must be born again, but He also explains to him what it means to be born again. Nicodemus initially found himself (just as many of us find ourselves concerning this very essential step in the salvation process) confused. He was an intelligent man who was highly educated in the law and in the early writings of the prophets, yet when Jesus says to him that if he wants to be with God he has to be reborn he is dumbfounded. The truth and power of Jesus' words land on eager yet ignorant ears. This further drives home the point that it doesn't matter how much Bible we know, what matters most is do we know God? And if we say we know God, then we will seek to live a life that pleases God. And we cannot please God unless we give up our life of sin and allow Him to rebirth within us a new life with new thoughts and new actions. We become a new man.

When we come into this world we are born with many traits and characteristics that are passed to us from our parents. The color of our eyes, hair, and skin are the gifts of our parents. Our height, muscle tone, and even athletic abilities have been attributed to heredity. Being born again means we will take on new characteristics; we will take on the characteristics of our father, God. No, it doesn't mean our hair color will change or that we'll grow 2 feet taller. But spiritually we will begin to look a lot like our Father. We will begin to love differently. We will begin to see things the way God does. We will become more compassionate for the lost. We will seek to do good and not evil. Our passions and desires will change from worldly lusts to heavenly priorities. We begin to look a lot like Jesus. Not the beard, robe and sandals but the obedience and submission to the Father. That is what being born again is all about. You are given a new life to live and this new life belongs to Christ who redeemed us. So live your life to please God and live your life as a thank you to Jesus.

REFLECT AND CONNECT

1. What is the dead give-away that a person has been born again?
2. When you become a born again believer, how do you think it will affect the direction of your life?
3. How would you explain what being born again means to a non-believer?

CONNECT WITH THE AUTHOR

Email me your questions or concerns about this chapter or share with me how this chapter blessed you.
got2liveright@gmail.com

Tell the world your thoughts about this chapter. Don't forget to mention me @ccody3 so I can connect with you.

CHAPTER 5

RESTORE

Restore unto me the joy of thy salvation; and uphold me with thy free spirit.
Psalm 51:12 KJV

The author of Psalm 51 knew very well the pain of being separated from God. At one point in his life, he had experienced an incredible closeness with God. In fact the Bible says that this man who penned these words was called "a man after God's heart". King David walked with God even at an early age. God had granted him one great success after another during this time. One of his earliest accounts of success was when God gave him the courage and strength to defeat the great giant Goliath in 1 Samuel. David knew what it meant to be "on top" with God. There was a time that David was so confident that all he had to do was ask and God would give. But as we read Psalm 51, it becomes apparent that something has taken place that has caused a need for restoration.

To be restored means to be put back to a former place, position, or rank. There was a time that man and God were close. In Genesis, God came down in the cool of the day to fellowship with Adam. God enjoyed those beautiful evenings and conversations with Adam. I can only imagine the serenity in the garden as God and Adam discussed the day. "What new animals have you named today, Adam? How do you like the taste of the fruit on the tree near the stream, Adam? Do you like the way those flowers look and smell, Adam?"

It was great being God's friend and companion, and then it happened! Sin reared its ugly head and ruined everything. The closeness that Adam experienced with God on a daily basis would be interrupted. Everything changed because of the one act of disobedience and rebellion. Thank God that this is does not have to be the end of the story. Because of Adam's rebellion, he needed to be redeemed. When Christ died on the cross, redemption was provided to every man who decides to repent. And if we repent and ask God into our hearts and ask Him to set us back on the path of righteousness and holy living, He will then restore us to our rightful place. We become sons of God. The garden experience can be ours once more. We no longer need to perform ritualistic sacrifices by killing doves, bullocks, and sheep. We no longer need to ask the Chief Priest to go into the most sacred part of the sanctuary to pray on our behalf. God restores us to the position that we first occupied. We can now be as close to God as we desire. So the question then becomes this: If we don't feel the closeness to God that we desire, what are we doing or NOT doing that is keeping that from happening?

People seem to always long for the "good ole days". With all of the advances that we experience in life why would someone want to go back to how things used to be? It is interesting how sometimes a new and supposedly improved product, idea, or method is not always the best product, idea, or method. If you were to ask most automobile enthusiasts, many will say that cars aren't built the way the used to be. If you were to consult with real estate agents, most would say that homes aren't built the way they used to be. There's something about the way things once were that people want to get back to. If you look around, you'll see old styles making a comeback. It is not uncommon to see hairstyles that were popular 20 to 30 years ago being requested in the salons today. The clothes that are purchased daily look very similar to the clothes that were worn two generations previously. There is something so sweet about going back to the way things once were. This is how God feels about our relationship with Him. He wants for us to rekindle the fire in our relationship with Him. He wants to restore within us the passion for living an upright and honorable lifestyle.

In Psalm 51:12, David asks God to restore the joy of his salvation. When we truly know God and have experienced an intimate relationship with God, but we allow sin to interrupt that connection, we will lose our joy. Life just doesn't seem to flow like it once did. Life isn't very pleasant any longer. We need to be restored. We need to be put back in our former position. God wants us to allow Him to return to His former position (Ruler of our hearts).

When the netbooks first hit the market, they became the next "big" thing because they were so small and compact. I just had to have one. In fact the first few chapters of the book that you are reading was written on my netbook. When I removed my beautiful black and sleek Gateway netbook from the box that it came in, I was excited. I couldn't wait to experiment with all of the options that this tiny computer had to offer. For a long time my netbook was perfect for me. It did everything I needed it to do and then one day my virus protection expired. My shiny and sleek tiny bundle of joy that I had come to love no longer had the protection that I once enjoyed. Because of this disconnection of service, my precious Gateway was exposed to a dreaded virus. It was much like this in the Garden of Eden. As long as Adam remained obedient to God, he enjoyed a connection with the Creator. This connection provided everything he needed, including protection. But when Adam found himself rebelling against God's rule, he also found himself disconnected from the One who provided protection. Sin ruined how everything functioned in the garden, just as the virus on my netbook ruined how my sweet Gateway functioned. I was once able to push the power button and within moments I had access to all that my computer offered. But now it took forever to get my computer to load. And then, once it did load, it was slooowwwwww. Pop-ups had made browsing the internet nearly impossible, because as I searched one website it seemed as though ten more sites were opening. So I cried out to my IT guy; my friend who seems to know everything about computers looked at my computer and uttered the words that I wasn't ready to accept. "If you want this computer to work like it did in the beginning, you'll need to restore it to the factory settings."

"What does that mean?" I asked in a depressed and saddened tone.

"You'll lose everything on your computer." He said with all the sympathy that he could muster.

"Everything? Is there any way I can save some of this stuff?" I asked hopefully.

"The problem is we don't know what is infected so it's best to just restore your computer and start over. It's like having a new computer."

Now those were words that made this process less painful. "It's like having a NEW computer." Who wouldn't want new if they could have it? I was now ready to give up the hope of holding onto all of my corrupted files. I was ready to start over fresh, to be new, to be perfect again. When the factory sent my computer out to the store to be sold, it was flawless. There was nothing wrong with it – no defects, no viruses, and no problems. You and I were the same way. When God made man, there was nothing wrong with man. He was God's perfect creation. God desires to restore all mankind to the position that we were created for. In order for this to take place we must admit that we need restoration and allow Him to remove all corruption from our lives. Let Him clean our hard drives (hearts) and remove all possible threats. And just like that, we become like new. "Therefore if any man be in Christ, he is a new creature: old things are passed away; behold, all things are become new." 2 Corinthians 5:17.

REFLECT AND CONNECT

1. If you don't feel as close to God as you'd like, what do you think is hindering the connection between you and God?
2. How does being disconnected from God leave you feeling? How does a strong connection with God leave you feeling?
3. Is there anything in your life that you're struggling to give up that is holding up the restoration process?

CONNECT WITH THE AUTHOR

Email me your questions or concerns about this chapter or share with me how this chapter blessed you.
got2liveright@gmail.com

Tell the world your thoughts about this chapter. Don't forget to mention me @ccody3 so I can connect with you.

CHAPTER 6

REJOICE

Rejoice in the Lord alway: and again I say, Rejoice.
Philippians 4:4 KJV

Rejoice! What thoughts or ideas does this mighty and powerful seven letter word bring to your mind? When you read it or when you hear it, doesn't the word just lift your spirit? Just uttering the word *rejoice* seems to make everything al right. To rejoice is to be happy or to take delight. So what is it that we have to be so happy about? Well, let's just take an inventory, shall we?

Everyone reading this book and even those who are not reading this book were all born with the same ending story: Eternal separation from God and eternal damnation in Hell. But that isn't the final chapter of your story, IF you don't want it to be. We do get to have a say, and we do have ultimate control over our final destination because of what God did for us through the sacrifice of Jesus Christ.

I think many Christians can go through life depressed and unenthused because they don't see all that they should be rejoicing about. One of the main strategies of the Devil is to distract us of what is most important. He attempts to keep us focusing on what we do not have in this world instead of looking at all that God has and is doing in our lives. Take away all of your material gain and earthly wealth and what do you have left? If you answer and say you've got Jesus, then you should be rejoicing. Rejoicing should be an automatic response every time you take a moment to ponder and realize that you do not have to die and go to Hell any longer.

Rebellion led to our need for redemption. God lovingly redeems all who will repent. Every man, woman, boy, and girl who confesses that Jesus is Lord and then turns away from sin and turns back to God is redeemed. When you accept Jesus' gift of redemption, then you will experience the rebirth. New life is found in Christ Jesus. Now we have a new way of doing things – The Kingdom's Way. God restores all those who are redeemed and reborn to the rightful position of a believer. You are now brought back in fellowship and communion with God. You now have access to everything God has access to. You can now reclaim your heavenly citizenship. If this doesn't call for rejoicing, I'm not sure anything would persuade us.

We should be overjoyed that a Holy and Mighty God loves us so much that He would go to great depths to save us. We should find ourselves weeping when we think about how unworthy we are and yet He loves us anyway. We should shout for joy when we think about how our past has been wiped away because Jesus' blood wipes away our sins. Are you not getting happier just thinking about how good God has been to you? Do you ever sit still and start rattling off all the things that you are thankful for? It will cause many of us to break down in tears of joy. Thank God for what He has brought you through. Thank God for what He has shielded you from. Thank God for the doors of opportunity that have been opened for you and for the doors of devastation and destruction that He slammed shut before any harm came over you. Aren't you happy you don't have to live this life alone? When you contemplate that He promises to be with us unto the end, does it make you want to praise God? When things get hard (and believe me they will), you are assured that God is still there. He tells us numerous times throughout the Bible that He will not abandon nor forsake us. Do these promises not make you want to find the highest rooftop and shout at the top of your voice, "THANK YOU, JESUS!"?

It is unfortunate that we take so many things for granted. The fact that we can breathe without trouble is reason enough to rejoice, but we keep breathing in and out like it's no big deal. We act as if this is not big enough to rejoice over. What will it take for it to become something we rejoice over? Does God have to revoke our oxygen privileges for us to rejoice over what He has given us? Does God have to step back and allow all manner of evil to strike at once for us to rejoice over His protecting hand? Why are our redemption and rebirth not something we cherish to a point that EVERY-TIME-WE-THINK-ABOUT-IT it makes us fall to our knees in gratitude?

Lord, I vow that I will show you honor by rejoicing over what some may call the "little things" of life. I have the movement of my limbs – I rejoice! I know my own name and where I live. I have the regulation of my mind – I rejoice! I may not have steak and lobster to eat, but I will not go hungry tonight – I rejoice! I might not have a Cadillac or Mercedes in my driveway. Wait, did I just say driveway? That means you've given me a place to live, Lord? So I rejoice! Again, I rejoice and again and again. God has been good to me, and God has been good to you, as well. So, there is but one response to such goodness – rejoice!

REFLECT AND CONNECT

1. What is one thing that God has done in your life that causes you to be grateful every time you think of it?
2. What have you taken for granted and not rejoiced over because you didn't see it as a big deal?
3. Is there anything in your life that is robbing you of your joy? Acknowledge it, bring it to God, and then leave it with Him.

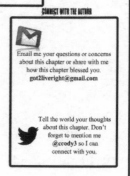

CONNECT WITH THE AUTHOR

Email me your questions or concerns about this chapter or share with me how this chapter blessed you.
got2liveright@gmail.com

Tell the world your thoughts about this chapter. Don't forget to mention me @ccody3 so I can connect with you.

CHAPTER 7

REPLACE

Replace: to put something new in the place of
Merriam-Webster Dictionary

If we have a choice of having something "like new" against having something brand new, more often than not we will select the thing that is brand new. There are no blemishes or wear and tear, no deterioration or reduction in quality. It's new, and we get to be the first to put it to use. I believe that it is God's greatest desire to replace our old heart with a new heart. God wants to give us a heart that seeks after Him and His righteousness. The problem is that our old heart beats to a rhythm that is anti-God. It has a selfish beat. Everything is about what we want and not what God wants. So repairing this heart is not an option for God. That old heart needs to be totally replaced. It needs to be removed, and another heart needs to be put in its place – a new one, one that hasn't been tarnished by the ways of the world. A heart that loves God for who He is and what He has done in our lives. A clean heart! In Psalm 51:10 David, after committing the terrible sin of adultery and then murder to hide his ungodly deeds, pens it perfectly, "Create in me a clean heart, O God; and renew a right spirit within me."

Allowing the "old" to remain and trying to refurbish it allows the flaws and weakness of the old to remain as well. In 2 Corinthians 5:17 Paul addresses the importance of walking in newness and doing away with the old things. "Therefore, if any man be in Christ, he is a new creature; old things are passed away; behold, all things are become new." When we realize our need of Jesus and we ask Christ into our hearts, He eagerly grants our request. He immediately gives us His Spirit. Operation Old Ways is activated and God immediately starts replacing things in our lives. Some things are replaced right away and some things are replaced through a process. The level of success that we will achieve in our Christian walk is hinged on our willingness to allow God to replace things that need to go and our not trying to hold onto things that aren't needed.

Our desire to hold on to baggage and our struggle to just let these things go reminds me of a television show called "Hoarders". The few times that I watched this show left me heartbroken and totally confused. Some people truly have a difficult time letting go of old stuff. Many of us who do not struggle with these types of problems will watch the show and begin judging the hoarder. The thing that saddens me most about the show is to watch the people who want to help them start over fresh with a new life and new beginning struggle to help them see their need to replace and discard all of that old stuff that is packed in their living room, dining room, kitchen, bedroom, garage, and any other space that something can fit. It is the same in our spiritual lives. We've got so much junk in our lives that there is no room for Jesus. Even though He is explaining to us that he wants to help us clean up all of the mess, we struggle to let Him replace the things in our lives that aren't needed. I have to confess that I've never made it through an entire episode because I get frustrated with the hoarder's unwillingness to let things go. Moving things around in the house wouldn't be enough. The things in that house need to be replaced. Moving things around in our lives is not enough; we need that stony heart of ours to be replaced with a heart that wants what God wants. "A new heart also will I give you, and a new spirit will I put within you: and I will take away the stony heart out of your flesh, and I will give you an heart of flesh." Ezekiel 36:26.

I remember a time when I walked into my house and the summer temperatures that I was trying to escape found their way into my home. I found myself thinking that there is NO way that I'm going to Hell. If I can't take these temperatures, I'm certain I can't handle Hell. I looked at the out of date thermostat on the wall and all of the settings were in the right place. The three knobs on the thermostat hadn't been altered; they remained on cool, auto, and 70 degrees, so I couldn't understand why my home felt like Satan's living room. The AC unit seemed to whine like my four year old as it continued working overtime to do what it was created to do. The unit was doing the best it could, but it could only muster the power to push out a sad amount of cool air and it struggled to take away the heat that was turning our home into our own personal sauna. I opened the grate that housed the filters and I immediately felt ashamed of myself as "The Man of the House". I remember thinking how the filter looked when I purchased it a couple months previously. It was whiter than Santa Claus's beard, but now both filters looked like they had been found in the Sahara Desert or in the remains of an ancient tomb. I think I could have made a queen-sized quilt with the dust and dirt that had accumulated over those past few months that would have given my super talented quilt-making grandmother a run for her money.

As much as my AC unit desired to do the best it could do its functioning was limited because the filters had to be replaced. Sure, I could take these filters outside and attempted to bang the dust off and hope that the unit would be restored to its full capability, but the results of this attempt would have only left me dusty and disappointed. If I wanted to get the best out of my AC unit, those filters would have to be removed and replaced. In like manner, the Lord has great things in store for His children but we cannot serve Him and give Him our best with an old dirty filter (heart). Until we allow Him to remove and replace the things in our lives that are hindering our efficiency as believers, we will continue to be weak, underachieving, and inefficient just like my unit. It is amazing how fast my home seemed to cool once the replacement was made. Ask yourself, what's in your life that needs to be replaced? What remains in your life that the Word of God speaks against? Are you holding on to things that are hindering you from becoming the man or woman that God wants you to be? If we ask God to show us anything and everything that remains in our lives that needs to be replaced, He will happily open our eyes to all things in our lives that need to be expelled.

In our lifetime we will have to replace many things. We'll have to replace the refrigerator or our food will spoil. We may have to replace a showerhead in the bathroom because of rust and calcium build up. If we own our car long enough, we may have to replace an engine in our car. If we want maximum comfort, we will have to replace the mattress in the bedroom. Why must these things be replaced? Why can't we make a minor repair and all is well again? Every believer must come to a point where we can see the big picture, the picture that God has painted. It's important to know that God is not interesting in us just "getting by" as churchgoers. He desires for us to triumph on our journey. He longs for us to be victorious in our Christian walk. There is absolutely no way we will be able to sustain this type of success if we are allowed to remain operating in our same old ways. Our motor (heart) must be replaced if we are going to make it down the road of life with the power that is needed to make this long haul. When we allow God to replace our old stony heart with a heart that seeks to please Him and live for Him, we *will* go from the little engine that could to the little engine that does.

RECAP

REFLECT AND CONNECT

1. What issues are you allowing to remain in your life that the Word of God speaks against?
2. What things are you holding on to that are hindering you from becoming the man or woman that God wants you to become?
3. If God were to reveal to you EVERYTHING He needed replaced in your life, would you submit to His will or would you resist?

CONNECT WITH THE AUTHOR

Email me your questions or concerns about this chapter or share with me how this chapter blessed you.
got2liveright@gmail.com

Tell the world your thoughts about this chapter. Don't forget to mention me @ccody3 so I can connect with you.

CHAPTER 8

REMEMBER

Remember: to keep in your mind; to not forget.
Merriam-Webster Dictionary

The Bible is filled with examples and accounts of a continuous cycle of mankind being blessed by God, forgetting what God had done for them in their past, and then returning to a lifestyle that displeases God. Often times when we read the Bible we are quick to judge these characters for their spiritual amnesia; however, if we were to truly examine our own lives we would certainly find times that we too forgot to include God in our decisions. We too have forgotten how good God has been to us. We too have forgotten that God deserves our praise regardless of the circumstances we find ourselves in. Remembering who God is and what He desires for our lives is essential if we are to have successful Christian lives.

Why is it so hard to remember certain things and yet not hard to remember others? Why can we remember a song we used to sing twenty years ago, but we cannot remember the passage of scripture from the pastor's sermon two hours ago? Are we wired to only remember certain things? Are our minds only capable of remembering a certain amount of data? Some have said that the human mind is like a sponge. It can soak up just about everything, but for some reason when it comes to the things of God our sponge seems to be a little less absorbent. Could it be that the most important thing for us to soak in and to absorb (the Word of God) is the thing we spend the least amount to time becoming familiar with?

We spend entirely too much of our time watching television, listening to music, or reading materials (newspaper, magazines, etc.) that don't have any positive influence on our lives. In contrast, the amount of time we spend reading our bibles, which can have a powerful influence in our lives, is minimal. It is because of this that we find remembering the things of God more difficult. The more exposure we have to the Word of God, the more difficult it will be for those life molding and life enhancing words to escape our thoughts. I am certain that most of us can readily remember a commercial we saw on television or a song we heard on the radio today or yesterday, but when we try to remember what passage of scripture we read last it seems to escape our thoughts.

If you were asked the question of which is most important in your life, God or your favorite television show or recording artist, I'm sure you would quickly reply that God is most important. If this is the case, why is it so hard for us to remember things that God says? I mean, why is the song so easy for me to remember? Why do I have no problem reciting every line in my favorite movie? The reasons are clear. 1) We enjoy the song and movie. We take delight in them and so we look forward to hearing or seeing them again. 2) We are exposed to them frequently. Most radio stations play the same songs over and over again. It can be overbearing if it's a song that you don't enjoy hearing. The crazy thing is that even that song that you don't like can become ingrained in your mind because of the continuous exposure you've had with the song. Have you ever caught yourself singing a song and then asked yourself: Why am I singing this stupid song? In the same way that we store and remember the words to those songs and lines in the movies, we can store and remember the Word of God. We must come to a point where we enjoy and delight in what the Bible has to say and teach. And we must increase our level of exposure to the Bible.

Things that we enjoy, we will remember. Psalm 119:1 says, "I will delight myself in thy statutes: I will not forget thy word." It is amazing how the more time we spend in the Word of God, the more we will come to enjoy the direction and protection that God offers through His Word. We will come to understand what the psalmist said in Psalm 119:103, "How sweet are thy words unto my taste! yea, sweeter than honey to my mouth!" We begin to love the Word and delight in the Bible's sweetness; when this happens it may seem like every little thing will trigger a memory of a verse that was sweet to us. The enemy will use every scheme and trick up his sleeve to keep us from developing a hunger and appetite for the sweetness of God's Word. Most of the times that we fall into temptation and sin are due to the limited time we invest in reading and studying the Word of God (Bible). The more Word we have stored within our hearts, the greater the chance that we will see through Satan's ploys and overcome the temptations that are placed on our path. Another nugget of wisdom I've gained from listening to my pastor speak was when he said, "Any place in your life that you have a weakness, find a scripture out of the Word of God that deals with that issue. So when temptation arises in our lives the scripture that you read, researched, remembered, and stored in your heart will rise up as well." When we've come to delight ourselves in God's Word, we won't forget the Word of God when we are under attack or under pressure in our daily lives.

Have you ever met someone for the first time, and when you walk away from him, you can't remember his name? How is that even possible? You were just speaking with him for thirty minutes and now you cannot remember what his name is. Did you ever park your car at the mall, and when you come out, you cannot remember where you parked? I recently watched a video posted on a social media site in which a lady recorded where she parked so she could locate her car when she was leaving her doctor's appointment. Apparently, she had lost her car the last time she was in that parking garage. How many of us have gone into the grocery store to get ONE item and when we leave we have 528 items and not one of them is that ONE item, we were sent to the store to purchase? We generally have these memory lapses because we aren't committed to the conversation with the person we're speaking with, or we aren't focused as we park our cars, or we weren't truly listening when our wife sent us to the store to buy that ONE ingredient to make the cake. The same thing happens to us spiritually. We aren't completely committed to the relationship we have with God, and because of this we will not remember the directions He has given us. The problem is that we haven't come to understand the value of those directions yet. We come to church, but our minds are at home or on some other adventure, and so we miss the message behind the message. We miss the still small voice of God trying to break the sermon down into a personal message tailored specifically for our lives. We hear and forget because we weren't really listening. The look of disappointment on the wife's face when you returned from the store without the item must be the look that God has on His face when we do not remember to do as He has instructed.

In 1 Chronicles 16:12 the Bible says, "Remember His marvelous works that He hath done, His wonders, and the judgments of His mouth." The Bible is a record of what God has done throughout the history of the world. It is filled with His marvelous works – from the moment He said, "Let there be light", in the beginning to the trumpet sounding at the second coming of Jesus Christ. If you were to read 1 Samuel 17, you would find one of my favorite stories – the story of David and Goliath. Most people have no problem remembering what God did for David and how He helped him defeat the great giant warrior. Everyone loves to root for the underdog, and the story of David's victory over Goliath is one of the greatest underdog stories ever recorded. This story was recorded to help us remember that with God nothing shall be impossible (Luke 1:37). David didn't fear the giant like all of the rest of the army men, but why? Where did his confidence come from? David remembered how God had been with him previously when he had to kill a bear and a lion that were trying to devour the sheep that were under his care. Remembering where God has brought us from and the deliverance that we've experienced in our past should build our confidence and faith in God. This confidence should motivate us to completely trust God and, more importantly, live the type of lives that please God. The story of David and Goliath helps us remember that in the same way that God could and did help David deal with the giants in his life, He'll help us deal with the giant obstacles in our lives. Years ago my pastor preached a message in which he said, "If we want what Abraham had, we must do what Abraham did!" How would we know what Abraham did if God didn't make sure it was recorded in the Bible to help us remember what He requires of those who follow Him and what it takes to gain His favor and blessings over our lives?

Sometimes we get so bogged down with life and we become so overwhelmed that we forget that we are the sons and daughters of the Living God. We allow the stresses and strains of life to smother the joy that God has given us. Another strategy our adversary (Satan) uses is distortion. His goal is to distort and invade our thoughts so that we do not remember what God has already done and what He promises He will do for His people. Sometimes we just need to sit still and reminisce. Just pause and ponder how God has been there for you in the past and what God has done in your life. Find a quiet place and just allow your thoughts to travel back in time and remember how God brought you out of that horrible situation or how God kept you from that devastating circumstance. I remember years ago while attending a worship service, one of the women became emotional and started to shout unto the Lord. She was crying and screaming "Thank you, Lord!" I remember thinking to myself that something was wrong with me. Why didn't I have that same passion? Why didn't I have that same praise in my heart? I prayed and asked God if I was lacking something in my relationship with Him. I asked Him why I didn't feel those same emotions. The answer I received continues to bless me to this very day. I heard a voice say to me, "You don't know what she has been through. You don't know what she has seen. So instead of waiting to praise me for bringing you out of a situation like hers, praise me that I've kept you away from situations that I allowed her to go through." That really blessed me. I've never forgotten that advice and I never will. So when you are sitting in your quiet space and you are meditating or remembering just how good God has been in your life, remember how He has kept you from enduring what many others have had to experience.

One Wednesday night during Bible study my pastor offered the congregation some great advice concerning spending more quality time with God. He said, "When you get in your car, DO NOT turn your radio on. Use your travel time as quiet time with God." This proved to be priceless advice for me. As I was riding to work one day in silence, the Holy Spirit flooded my thoughts with the things of God. So when you find your quiet place, just think about how that sermon that you really needed to hear came right on time. Ponder the times that you heard the Spirit speak in your ear and how each time you honored the advice of the Spirit things worked out in your favor. Contemplate the time you knew for sure that you wouldn't make it through tomorrow and that tomorrow was nearly ten years ago! God is good, and He deserves our praise and obedience. If we can slow down and just remember who we are in Christ, we will be able to refocus ourselves and remain on the course that He's placed us on.

REFLECT AND CONNECT

CONNECT WITH THE AUTHOR

Email me your questions or concerns about this chapter or share with me how this chapter blessed you.
got2liveright@gmail.com

Tell the world your thoughts about this chapter. Don't forget to mention me @ccody3 so I can connect with you.

1. Pray and ask God to speak to your mind. Grab a sheet of paper; set a timer for five minutes. Write down as many situations as you can remember where God was there for you.
2. Can you remember a time where you felt God guiding yet felt the enemy distracting at the same time? Which voice did you honor? Do you remember how you felt after you won or lost that battle to temptation?
3. How much time per day or week do you spend reading the Bible? (Challenge: spend five minutes in prayer, ten minutes reading the Bible, and five minutes in closing prayer daily.)

CHAPTER 9

RESIST

It's easier to resist at the beginning than at the end.
Leonardo da Vinci

We tend to resist the words and direction of the One that we should embrace and we embrace and adhere to the words of the one that we should resist. To resist is to take a stand or make an effort in opposition. Why would anyone choose to oppose God? Why do we resist His guidance and His ways? Many times God's commands and His ways are so fundamentally opposite of our natural inclinations that our first instinct is to resist the instructions and fight against the change that He calls for in His followers. "For my thoughts are not your thoughts, neither are your ways my ways, saith the LORD" (Isaiah 55:8). God is not surprised that our initial responses to His commands are usually responses of resistance. It is something that He has endured from Mankind since the beginning. "Ye stiffnecked and uncircumcised in heart and ears, ye do always resist the Holy Ghost: as your fathers did, so do ye." (Acts 7:51)

It is vital that we spend quality time with God. This will help us to continue remembering what God has done for us. That quiet time with God will conjure up the memory of our rebellion and then His redemption that we didn't deserve. We'll think about the time we broke down in tears and repented and told God that we wouldn't continue to live in sin. We'll have the opportunity to remind ourselves that we've been reborn and that God has restored us to our rightful position in the family of God. This quality time will build up our courage to trust God more and stop resisting Him.

Another one of my favorite Bible stories is the story of Jonah and the great fish. Jonah was a prophet of God, but even Jonah found himself resisting God's plans and rebelling against God's directions. God gave Jonah a very important mission. It was a dangerous mission and it was a mission that Jonah didn't want to accept. God told Jonah to go to the city of Nineveh and tell the people of that wicked city that He would destroy them if they didn't turn from their wickedness and turn to God. This city was a very lawless and ungodly city. Ninevites didn't know God and didn't love God like Jonah and his people did. Jonah knew of their reputation and how these people didn't particularly care for his people. He knew that this mission could very quickly go awry. Jonah knew that if they wanted to they could kill him as soon as he entered their gates and opened his mouth. Jonah's resistance is not much different from the resistance we often display toward God. Just as he ran – we run. God said go this way and he went that way. Often times God tells us to go a certain way and we choose to go in the opposite direction just as Jonah did. We resist the God who has done nothing but bless and keep us. We turn our backs on the God who has delivered us time and time again. We run away from Him instead of running into His arms. But why would we resist God? "He knows everything and He can be trusted." These words or words similar to these have left our lips on many occasions when we wanted people to see how "religious" we are. But when the tough task is handed down to us, we become the Jonah of the day – we run and we resist.

Because we don't always see the big picture, we often times find ourselves hesitant and resistant when it comes to obeying the commands of God. But if we really do trust God, there is no need to resist. In time, all of us will come to realize and understand that it's futile to resist God. Jonah's story vividly makes this point crystal clear. Jonah ran to the port and found a boat going as far away from God's commands as possible and paid his fees to ride that boat. When the ship got out into deep waters, a hurricane like storm started to brew. The Bible gives us to know that the experienced crew began to panic. Whenever I read about their panic, I can imagine just how powerful this storm must have been. No doubt these men have been in storms in the past, but this one was different. They were afraid for their lives. They didn't think they'd make it out of this storm. Jonah revealed to them why they were in the storm and instructed them to throw him over if they wanted to survive. I've always wondered why Jonah didn't just jump in himself. Sometimes we just need to be pushed.

"Now the LORD had prepared a great fish to swallow up Jonah. And Jonah was in the belly of the fish three days and three nights." (Jonah 1:17) The NIV translation uses the word *provided* in the place of *prepared* found in the King James translation. I love the word provided. God provides just what we need to come to ourselves and to realize it is no use resisting Him. We may as well just do what God tells us to do. Life is easier that way. God gives us clear and direct instructions for our lives, but if we resist we may find ourselves in the same predicament as Jonah. Maybe you don't get swallowed by a fish and have to remain in its belly for three days but maybe you have to go to prison for 10 years for your resistance. Maybe you have to remain in an ungodly and horrible marriage because you resisted God's instructions about being unequally yoked with an unbeliever. Maybe you have to endure the results of the STD you contracted at the age of 15 because you resisted the instructions of God and lived a promiscuous lifestyle. Let me see if I can make all of this make sense in 6 words: IT DOESN'T PAY TO RESIST GOD!

Okay, now that we've looked at who we shouldn't resist, let's look at who and what we should resist. "Submit yourselves, then, to God. Resist the devil, and he will flee from you" (James 4:7). It all starts with submitting ourselves to God. Submit has become a word that we don't like to speak unless it benefits us, unless we are trying to get someone to submit to us. Husbands are quick to quote Ephesians 5:22 when we want control, "Wives, submit yourselves unto your own husbands, as unto the Lord." But there is a reason much deeper and richer for these instructions. These words were not penned to give the man the ability to abuse and dominate his family, but they were recorded because God knows that if resistance is allowed to reside in our homes, we will not be able to build the type of godly homes that will show the world who God is. If we are going to have the strength and ability to resist the devil and all that he tries to perpetrate in our lives, we're going to have to first pledge allegiance to God. As we build a relationship with God, we will come to understand that the devil actually has no power over us. But until we establish a relationship with God and grow closer to Him, we have no power to overpower the bluff of the devil. The devil has a great poker face, but when we have Jesus in our hearts and we allow the Holy Spirit to guide our lives, we have all the cards in our favor. It saddens me to hear so many Christians use the excuse, "We are only human," to justify our weaknesses and our caving into temptation and giving into the devil's plots and schemes.

God would never require us to do something that He has not provided the ability or power to do. So when He instructs us to resist the devil and to not cave into temptation, it is because He has given us the power to do just that. When Jesus rose from the dead after staying in the tomb for three days, He snatched all of the power from sin and death. At that very moment sin could no longer rule us IF we didn't want it to. If we want to resist and win, we can! The main reason that we find ourselves failing to remain victorious over sin is that we haven't mastered the first portion of James 4:7. We haven't learned to completely submit ourselves to God and allow Him to teach us how to carry out the mission of holy living.

The Bible tells us in Ephesians 6:12, "For we wrestle not against flesh and blood, but against principalities, against powers, against the rulers of the darkness of this world, against spiritual wickedness in high places." There is a war going on for our souls. I've always found it amazing that the Lord doesn't tell us that we have to fight. He tells us to just resist the enemy. He tells us that the battle is His, but we do have a part in the battle. We must resist! Jesus modeled for us exactly how to put James's words into action. He lays out the game plan for us to follow in order to resist the devil. He shows us that it is true that if we stay strong and continue to resist, the devil will leave us alone. In Matthew 4:1-11, Jesus is led by the Spirit into the wilderness where He fasted and prayed. The devil shows up at the end of Jesus' fast and tries to tempt Jesus to go against God's plans in order to satisfy His own personal agendas and needs. Jesus had been out in the wilderness for 40 days. He had spent 40 days without food and he dedicated that time to getting closer to His Father. Can you imagine going 40 days without food! Most of us struggle to go 40 minutes without food (another lesson in which resistance could lead to blessings). The devil comes to Jesus at an ideal time to try and throw Jesus off the path. He knew that Jesus must be very hungry and so he tries to persuade Jesus to turn the stones into bread and eat. What should we take from these verses? We'd better believe that the enemy knows exactly when to show up in our lives to try and throw us off the course that God has us on. Jesus' response was to tell the devil exactly what God says in the Word of God. The devil isn't one to give up easily. He tries 2 more times and uses 2 more schemes to get Jesus to lose focus on His mission. Each time Jesus remains strong, speaks the Words of God over the situation, and resists the devil's attempt. After the devil tried the third time, he realizes that Jesus wasn't going to give in and so he left Jesus alone. If we stay strong, stay in the Word, and stay focused on our mission from God, the devil will flee from us as well.

As Leonardo da Vinci said, "It's easier to resist at the beginning than at the end." If we give in from the start, the devil is going to fight with all that he has to make sure we don't get back to God. It's best if we just make up our minds that we belong to God from the beginning, to start building our relationship with God and storing as much of God's Word in our hearts for when the enemy comes to attack us. He will come in the moments when we are weak and he will attempt to persuade us to go after what we want and not what God wants. At that time we've got to use the model that Jesus left for us and resist all of the devil's tricks. If we submit ourselves to the Lord, we will find the strength we need within ourselves to resist and win!

REFLECT AND CONNECT

1. Do you find that you are more submissive or resistive toward God?
2. Do you believe that you have the power to defeat temptation every time it comes?
3. What steps do you take to overcome temptation when you battle the desire to do the wrong things?
4. Grab a mirror, look directly at yourself, and say this statement three times, "If I submit to God, I will have the power to resist the devil. If I resist the devil, he will leave me alone and I will walk in victory."

CONNECT WITH THE AUTHOR

Email me your questions or concerns about this chapter or share with me how this chapter blessed you.
got2liveright@gmail.com

Tell the world your thoughts about this chapter. Don't forget to mention me @ccady3 so I can connect with you.

CHAPTER 10

REMAIN

remain: to stay in the same place or with the same person or group; to stay after others have gone
Merriam-Webster Dictionary

After we've acknowledged our need for God and have repented and come back home, we need to remain with Him. We need to stay put. We must stay with God and among the people of God if we are going to remain on the path that God calls us to. If we remain in Christ, we will not be able to remain the same. There will be constant and consistent improvement in our lives. We tend to fall back into the bad habits of our old lifestyle when we don't remain in Christ.

REMAIN IN CHRIST

What do I mean when I say remain in Christ? I mean staying close to Him and staying connected to Him. We never leave His side. A wonderful promise that we can all stand on is that God never abandons the relationship that we have with Him. So if there is ever a disconnection or a problem in our relationship with God, it is because we have chosen not to remain with

Christ. We've chosen to step away. We've chosen to see what the world has to offer. It is ironic that when God tells us to remain, to stay put, to stand still and see the salvation of the Lord (Exodus 14:13), it is then that we have the hardest time remaining where He instructs us to stay. However, when He tells us to go, to move, to advance, it is then that we want to remain where we are.

God had promised the Children of Israel a land flowing with milk and honey. He promised them a life of abundance. Moses, the leader of God's people, sent spies to scope out the new land that God was going to give them, and when their reports poured in about how wonderful the land was and all that was there to be enjoyed, the people became excited. God had promised them this land, but there was a problem. There were giants in the land. God's chosen people would rather remain where they were instead of trusting God and moving forward as God had instructed. It is not uncommon for believers today to possess the same mindset as the Israelites did in our bible stories. We don't mind following God when everything is favorable and easy, but as soon as there is a little opposition or when things get a little harder than we anticipated, we struggle to remain faithful in following God's directions.

We will never become the men and women that God wants us to be if we cannot remain faithful to the plans that He has for our lives. Just as water will never become ice if it doesn't remain in the freezer, we will never experience the fullness of God's promises if we refuse to remain in Christ in spite of what the circumstances of life appear to be. Another trick of the devil is to distort our vision of God's plans for our lives so that he can convince us that remaining faithful and committed to God is profitless. But only after the water has endured the cold and harsh temperatures as it remained in the freezer does it become a cube or block of ice. Now it can be used for things that water can't be used for. Something we must always remember is that if God calls us to do or be something, He makes all arrangements for those orders to be carried out but the only way to accomplish God's will and God's work in our life is to remain in Christ.

In the Bible the word *abide* is synonymous with the word *remain*. In John 15:4-5 the bible says, "Abide in me, and I in you. As the branch cannot bear fruit of itself, except it abide in the vine; no more can ye, except ye abide in me. I am the vine, ye are the branches: He that abideth in me, and I in him, the same bringeth forth much fruit: for without me ye can do nothing." We can't do anything without God. We can't become who we are capable of becoming if we don't abide, if we don't remain. If we want to be productive and continue to be fruitful in our life's journey and if we want to experience true success (living a full life with purpose) we must abide; we must remain in Christ.

REMAIN FOCUSED

Another of my favorite stories in the Bible is the story of Peter walking on water with Jesus. In this story Peter and the other disciples are out on the sea when Jesus starts to walk out to them. At first they don't recognize

Jesus and they become frightened because they assume He is a ghost. Jesus calms their fears by letting them know that it is Him and that they have no need to be troubled. Upon hearing Jesus' words, Peter immediately asks to come out on the water to join Jesus.

What I've always loved about this story was that Jesus didn't tell Peter that he wasn't ready for that type of experience. His response to Peter's request is the same response He has for all of Mankind, "Come."

When Peter steps out of the boat, something unbelievable happens. In my imagination I can see it vividly. As his feet touches the cool and refreshing waters, only the bottoms of his feet seem to be getting wet. Peter looks down and notices the impossible happening right before his very eyes and right below his feet. He is actually standing on top of the water! He takes one step and then another and to his surprise he is still on top. I can just see the smile on his face and I can hear the pounding of his heart. With every step he takes, his smile gets bigger and his heartbeat settles. What started as disbelief has now become his expectation. He expects his next step to be sure. He expects to stay on top of the water. When we follow the voice and direction of Jesus, we can have the confidence that Peter possessed. When we hear Jesus tell us to come, we too can step out of the boats of our lives and expect each step to be secure.

The amazement of the situation must have been overwhelming for the other men in the boat as well. They were all watching and anticipating how everything would play out. In our day and time, each disciple would have quickly pulled out his cellphone and started recording this awesome display of God's power, ready to post their footage on various social media sites and grab a million views overnight.

Peter's fear fades and he starts making his way toward Jesus. He no longer finds himself wondering if the water will hold him up because he is completely and totally focused on his teacher who is standing in front of him. He continues taking steps to get closer to Jesus when all of a sudden a storm rises on the waters. Isn't that how it normally goes? When you are truly focused on getting closer to Christ don't be surprised when storms will arise.

As believers we must constantly remind ourselves that the enemy will try to cultivate storms in our lives to distract us so that we take our focus off Jesus. If our focus is taken off Christ even for just a moment, we may find ourselves sinking in the same situations that we used to easily walk through. Peter had just experienced something that only two men have ever done, but because he couldn't remain focused on Christ in the time of the storm he lost his ability to stay on top. No matter what comes up in our lives, we must remain focused on Jesus. When storms arise in your life, tell yourself that if Jesus called you to the task He will make sure you can perform that task. No matter what rises up against you, just keep your eyes on Him. One of the most discouraging and heartbreaking things we see among those that claim to be believers is that when things in life become hard or when storms are overtaking us, it is then that we tend to look back and look away from Christ.

The Bible doesn't say it, but in my imagination I can see this intense situation play out. I can hear the dialogue between Peter and Jesus. Peter's faith is being strengthened with every step that he takes on top of the water, but now it is fading fast with every moment that the storm brewed. The volume of the wind's howl startles Peter and although Peter had navigated the seas since he was old enough to walk onboard a ship, he'd never seen waves like these. Peter's faith is taking leave and his fear is taking command. The others on the boat scream out to Peter pleading with him to get back in the boat. Peter doesn't know if he should keep going toward Jesus or strive to make it back to the security of the vessel. As the wind's howl rapidly increases, Peter finds himself becoming paralyzed with fear. The water that was first cooling the bottoms of his feet has now become waves that are slapping against his upper legs. His heart rate is through the roof. The intensity of the pounding has radiated from his chest to his ears as he can now hear his heart enter survival mode! And then Jesus speaks.

"Peter, look at me! Peter focus on me!"

"But Jesus, the storm! The wind is so loud; the waves are so big!"

"Peter, look at me! I've got you, Peter. Just keep walking towards me."

"Jesus, I'm scared." The wind's hiss grows louder attempting to drown out Jesus' words.

"Peter, I've got you. Don't worry about anything but walking to me. Don't listen to the wind. Don't look at the waves. Just focus on me."

"But Jesus…" he barely gets the words out when he realizes that his foot is starting to go under. Once we lose focus on Christ, doubt then overtakes us, and when doubt is present it will rob us of seeing and experiencing what God can do in our lives.

"Peter, just breathe! Look at me. Look at me. Focus on my voice. Focus on my instructions."

Peter begins to sink completely. He is an experienced fisherman and knows how to swim. But the storm has interfered with his ability to focus on anything but the storm. Water fills his mouth as the waves rush over him as he tries to scream out for Jesus. The men in the boat try desperately to get to him, but the wind and waves are such a powerful opposition that they render their efforts completely futile. No matter how hard they row, they aren't getting any closer to Peter. If anyone could save Peter, it would have to be Jesus, and if anyone can save us, it will have to be Jesus, for Jesus is the only one who can save.

"Jesus, help me! Lord, save me!" Peter manages to force the words out in between the assault of each violent wave. Perhaps the part of this story that I love the most happens next. This scene takes place in Matthew 14:31. The Bible says that after Peter cried out for the Lord to save him, "Immediately Jesus reached out his hand and caught him." I've always loved that the Bible says that Jesus reached out His hand, not his arm, and not a rope.

His hand tells me that Peter was almost there. Many times we are so close to Jesus when we lose focus and start to sink and drown in the storms of life. When the storms of life arise, we must remember that we shouldn't focus on the storm, but rather we should focus on the One who can calm the storm with just a few words, "Peace be still." (Mark 4:39)

REMAIN FAITHFUL

I'll never forget the conversation I had with a colleague at work several years ago. Her role as a guidance counselor always gave me comfort in seeking her advice about certain matters. Her schooling and training equipped her with wisdom and knowledge on a vast array of life's issues. She always impressed me with her knowledge of how our students thought and why students behaved in the manner that they did. On this particular day the topic of our conversation was marital infidelity. I asked her, "What percentage of married men do you think cheat on their wives?" Without batting an eye or taking a moment to contemplate the question she answered emphatically, "I say about 90 percent of married men cheat on their wives."

"90 percent!" I quickly said in total disbelief. My brain couldn't wrap around the idea of 9 out of 10 married men stepping out on their wives. She didn't budge or waver as I continued to dispute and challenge her logic. I began to rattle off names of the male teachers in the school who were married. After every name I mentioned, she would confidently state that she believed that those men had been unfaithful. And then she asked me what percentage of married men did I think were unfaithful. I told her that I figured it was around 30 percent. I just couldn't bring myself to accept that 90 percent of men couldn't remain faithful to their wedding vows. Then she told me to go home and ask my wife what she thought. I cut her off as I answered for my wife, "She'll say about 30 percent just like I do, or maybe she'll say 40 percent but no more than that." She smiled and repeated the instructions to ask my wife her opinion.

When I got home that evening, my wife and I were discussing our day when the discussion between me and my colleague came up. I asked my wife the same question that was posed earlier in the guidance office. "What percentage of married men do you think cheat on their wives?" I immediately stuck my chest out as I awaited my wife's answer. I know my wife so well. I know that she and I think alike. Well, those were the thoughts that rushed through my mind. My wife (just as my friend earlier in the day) didn't need time to think. No moment was needed to ponder the questions. She immediately blurted out, "I'd say about 90 percent."

"What!" I said in disbelief. How could she believe such a thing. "You mean to tell me that you believe 9 out of 10 married men cheat on their wives?"

"The worst part is how many of us think that our husbands are in that 10 percent who will remain faithful." Her answer caught me off guard. How could these two very intelligent women think so lowly of men? How could they even for one moment assume so many couldn't remain faithful? Their life experiences had shown them that faithfulness is something that is fleeting and almost a far-fetched concept.

We live in a world where faithfulness is not the norm. The movies and television shows that we watch are filled with infidelity. The music that is poured into our ears bombards us with the concept that one woman or one man just isn't enough. Faithfulness seems to be found only in a few. But why is this? What has happened? One word: Sin. Unfaithfulness is not a new problem. It's not a 21st century issue. From the bedroom to the boardroom, unfaithfulness has been the cause of many major break-ups throughout history.

Being faithful is what we are called to be because God is faithful. God has not left us and promises to NEVER leave or forsake us. It is Mankind, who have been unfaithful to God. This, too, is not a new problem. Man has been unfaithful to God from the beginning and this problem continues today. But how could we not be faithful to the best thing in our lives? I think this is the same question that many wives and husbands ask when they find that their spouse is having an affair. "What's wrong with me? Why are you doing this to me? Have I not been a good husband or a good wife? How could you throw away what we have for a few moments of pleasure?"

Oftentimes people are unfaithful because they are not satisfied with their current situation. But if we can't find satisfaction in God, it is probably because we have never truly met God. We've never truly come to know

Him. Sure, we've gone to church our whole lives and we've even sung in the choir and taught Sunday School, but maybe we've never established a real relationship with God. And the first "pretty thing" that the world has to offer us easily pulls us away from our so-called commitment to God. I believe that many of us don't remain faithful to God because we don't realize what we really have with God. We don't see what a relationship with God really means. We struggle to grasp the depth of the sacrifice that Jesus made on our behalf and all of the love that He's poured into the relationship. In my opinion, it is impossible to truly understand what He has done for us and not love and cherish Him. It is hard to cheat on God with this dirty and deceitful world when we really understand how much He actually loves us.

One of the stories in the Bible that had always intrigued me is found in Hosea. God instructs the prophet Hosea to marry a specific woman. Doesn't sound too interesting yet, right? Well, look a little deeper. The woman that God tells this man of God, this preacher, this prophet who delivers His words to the world, to marry is a harlot (a prostitute). Whoa! Back up! God would never tell a preacher to marry a woman who has this type of reputation, right? Wrong! God was going to use this man's relationship with his wife to illustrate to the entire nation how they treated or rather how they mistreated God. After marrying the prophet, this woman eventually returns to her old ways of living, but God instructs him to go and get her back and bring her back home. God instructs Hosea to remain faithful even though she is unfaithful.

Does this sound familiar? We've all been like Hosea's wife. We've all been unfaithful to God even though He has done nothing but been a good provider and protector for us. Because He loves us so much, He is willing to go after us to bring us back home. When Jesus came to this earth to take on the sins of the world, He was doing the same thing Hosea did. He was coming to reclaim his bride and bring her back home. I am so grateful that although I've not always been faithful to God, He has always remained faithful to me. God's faithfulness motivates me to remain faithful to Him.

If we are going to remain faithful, we must be aware and alert to the fact that the world is going to try its best to entice us to leave God. The world is going to show us its beauty and all that it can offer if we'll just step away from God and spend a little time with it. But the world is NOT going to show us its crazy side. The world won't reveal to us that it has destructive and evil motives. We generally find that out when it's too late to do something about it. When I was a young man I saw a movie that scared me away from marital unfaithfulness. The movie was the Hollywood blockbuster *Fatal Attraction*. In this movie a savvy business man finds himself in the arms of another women when his wife is out of town. This woman caught his attention and nearly derailed his life. She was beautiful, she said the right things, she offered him an exciting weekend of pleasure but what came next was eye opening. She was possessive! She wanted more than that one weekend of fun. She wanted him to leave his family and be with her and she wasn't willing to take no for an answer. In the end the lady had to be killed because she came into their home seeking to kill and destroy his family.

Sin isn't going to show you that it is just like the unstable woman in this movie. Sin won't show you that if you choose to spend the weekend with her that she won't rest until she pulls you away from your God and if that means destroying you and everything connected to you, then so be it. The best way to remain faithful is to constantly remind yourself of what you have with God. Remind yourself how much He loves you and how no one has ever loved you like this and no one ever will. Remind yourself of what you've been through with God. Remind yourself of the time and energy you've invested in your relationship with God and, more importantly, the time and blessings that He's invested in you. And when this doesn't push the temptation to cheat on God out of your mind, remind the enemy of his destiny and remind him that it is because of his choice to be unfaithful to God.

REMAIN "FIRED UP"

It is difficult to remain focused and faithful when we allow our fire for Christ and the things of God and His kingdom to dwindle. Keeping the passion burning in our spiritual relationship is what aids us in staying focused and staying faithful. Just as in marriage, men and women for ages have stated that the reason that they stepped outside their covenant promise to remain faithful is that they didn't "feel the fire" any longer. The passion was gone. The thrill was missing. The fire had dwindled. If we are going to live for God in a manner that pleases Him, we must keep our fires burning by throwing more logs of love unto the fire. We must never let the love we have for God flicker like a candle.

When I was a teenager, there was a very popular video game that we played called NBA JAM. It was a 2 on 2 basketball game where you could select 2 players from your favorite NBA team. If one of the players made several shots in a row, the announcer would say, "He's heating up!" And if he made one more shot without the opposing team scoring, the announcer would then shout, "He's on fire!" Once your player was ON FIRE, everything he shot seemed to go in. HE COULDN'T MISS! It was so awesome to see his shots scorch the nets and burn them up. His consistency in game play led to him HEATING UP. His diligent play pressed him even further until he was deemed ON FIRE. Now he was literally unstoppable. In our walk with God we also have the opportunity to catch fire and do miraculous things, but in order for that to happen, we must remain focused and faithful in the game called Life. The reason many believers are NOT achieving the greatness that they are capable of and the reason that many believers are NOT catching and keeping the fire is that many believers have very little commitment to stick with God when things get tough. As soon as we miss a few shots in life we tend to give up or abandon the game plan that God has laid out for us. Our fires fade quickly in the sight of adversity or as soon as God doesn't give us our way.

In Leviticus chapter 6, the Lord gave Moses instructions to give to the priests concerning the offerings that were conducted upon the altar. In verse 13, God commands that the fire that burned upon that altar must NEVER go out. It should always be burning. Every day the priests were to add wood to the fire to ensure that the fire didn't fade. Every day we are to add wood from the Word of God to our fires to ensure our fires don't fade either. Each day we should awake with a passion to serve God. We should arise with a prayer on our lips and joy in our hearts. We should seek God immediately for the day's orders and commands. We should have a scheduled devotional time with God. This will give us some much needed logs to keep our fires burning for this day. If we don't throw those logs on the altar of our hearts quickly, the devil will do all that he can to interrupt our day and keep us from kindling the fire. The thing to remind ourselves is that it doesn't take long for the fire to fade, but it often takes long to get it restarted. The key is to never let it go out.

There are several things that you can easily add to your everyday routine (a word I hate to use when talking about the things of God) to help keep your fire burning or to help you remain fired up. If you truly desire to remain fired up for God, here are three areas of advice to follow:

    1. You need to pray every day. You cannot maintain a passionate relationship with anyone you don't

spend time talking to. It's interesting how when we first start dating someone, we spend hours upon hours on the phone with him or her. It may be 2:00 or 3:00 in the morning and neither person wants to hang up although both are struggling to hang in there on the phone. If we want to get closer to God, we are going to have to spend more time talking with Him. There is plenty to talk about, but more importantly there is plenty that He'd like to say to us. Remember – prayer is NOT a one way communication line. If we allow God to speak during our prayer time, He will tell us what we need to hear and do in order to continue to live a life that is upright, holy, and pleasing unto Him.

2. You need to read your Bible every day. The Bible is God's words to us. It is His instructions and His law. It is a manual that all believers can use to strengthen their relationship with God and with one another. It is a powerful book, filled with wonderful words of encouragement, enlightenment, and love. When we open the Bible and begin to read it, we will find the guidance we need to help us avoid burn-out as believers. The Word of God, when it is read and applied, tends to set us ablaze with zeal and passion for the things of God. Unfortunately, a steady dose of the Bible is one of the ingredients that is missing in most of our lives. We don't mind praying or singing, but to sit down and spend time reading seems to be asking for too much. However, it is through the reading

of God's Word consistently and purposefully that we find the very logs that will keep our fires blazing. Our lives will put off so much light and heat that we will begin to impact the lives of others. People will either come closer to be warmed or move away because the truth is too hot to handle. And you know what they say, "If you can't handle the heat, then get out of the kitchen." So it becomes necessary for us to develop a plan for reading the Bible or a schedule to follow. One of the greatest bits of advice that my pastor gave our church about Bible reading and staying strong is to admit the areas of weakness in our lives and then find as many verses as possible on that topic and begin reading those. When you follow this advice, you will begin to see tiny sparks (sparks of love, hope, and encouragement); then those sparks will begin to land in your life and then ignite your life, and before you know it, the heavenly commentators will announce, "YOU'RE ON FIRE!"

3. You've got to meditate. When I say meditate, I'm not speaking of some chanting in a corner. Meditation is thinking intently on the words that you read and the words that you prayed. Allow the words you read and prayed to invade your mind and control your thought process. Let them flood your mind like that song that you can't force out of your thoughts no matter how hard you try.

The things that we tend to spend time thinking about are the things that eventually rule our lives. Allow that scripture that you just read concerning submission or the one about guarding your tongue and valuing the words that you allow to escape your lips continue to play through your mind. Visualize yourself going through scenarios where you put those words into action. See yourself successfully following God's instructions. You will find a new appreciation for the way in which God's guidance makes life sweeter and easier. And the end result usually leads to a brighter and hotter fire in your life.

REFLECT AND CONNECT

1. How would you explain to someone what it means to remain in Christ?
2. Can you pinpoint anything in your life that is robbing you of your ability to focus on God and His will for your life?
3. Think back to when you first gave God your heart. Can you remember how in love you felt? What do you think it would take for you to get back to that?

CONNECT WITH THE AUTHOR

Email me your questions or concerns about this chapter or share with me how this chapter blessed you.
got2liveright@gmail.com

Tell the world your thoughts about this chapter. Don't forget to mention me @ccody3 so I can connect with you.

CHAPTER 11

RESPOND

respond: to do something as a reaction to something that has happened or been done; to have a particular reaction to something.
Merriam-Webster Dictionary

There are always two ways to respond to every question or every situation. We can respond with a YES or we can respond with a NO. When it comes to our spiritual lives it is no different. We can respond to God and His goodness with a YES response or we can give Him the cold shoulder with our NO response. One of the concepts that must be understood is that by not responding to God with a YES, we are in fact giving God a NO response. It's hard to believe that we would ever respond with a NO after reading about what God has done and who God is. Or to make it more personal or bring it closer to home, when we look at our own lives and how God has been there for us day after day, it's hard to believe that "Yes, Lord" isn't the only answer that we can muster.

In the beginning of this book you read where man rebelled against God. So how did God respond to man's decision to do his own thing and ruin the plans that God had in place? HE DIED FOR MAN! Through the life and death of Jesus, God responds to the separation between Him and man. After Jesus rose from the grave, man could now respond to God with a YES and respond to sin with a NO. We have a choice as to how we will respond to every situation that comes our way. This is what many call "Free Will." God doesn't force us to respond to Him in a favorable manner, but He hopes that, as we come to know Him, our responses will always be that of trust, reliance, and obedience.

Many of us hate change. In fact we generally respond to change by resisting it. We fight against change even though the change is desperately needed. It is important to know that we cannot serve God and remain in relationship with Him if we don't change our ways. The blessing of serving God is that He is understanding and compassionate. He knows that we have lived in sin for many years and that it may take time for us to learn, accept, and then live our lives in a totally new and different way. But if our response to change is always resistance, we will never become the men and women that Jesus died to empower us to be. Our response toward change must be embraced. Our willingness to lean on and trust God becomes our normal response, our daily response, when we pause and think about what God has done for us even when we didn't know or worship Him. In Romans 12:2, the Bible says, "And be not conformed to this world: but be ye transformed by the renewing of your mind, that ye may prove what is that good, and acceptable, and perfect, will of God." The word *transformed* means to change. Our response to God for His saving grace should be a changed life – a holy life. One of the first responses that we must make is to change the way we think (renewing our minds). In a letter that Paul writes to the Philippian church, he explains exactly what type of mindset they needed to adapt and those words of advice and encouragement apply to our lives as well. "Let this mind be in you, which was also in Christ Jesus." (Philippians 2:5)

Our mindsets will determine how we respond to everything. Our responses toward life's issues will be handled differently when we have the mindset of Christ. We will see the world through a different lens when we are led by the mind of Christ. Shortly after the tragedies of 9/11, an NFL player with the Arizona Cardinals, named Patrick Tillman, decided to leave the glory of the football field to become a soldier on the battlefield. His mindset toward his country motivated him to enlist in the U.S. Army. Not everyone had that same response, because not everyone had his mindset. Our response is always connected to what we are committed to. Our response is always connected to what we have a passion for. So when we respond to God with obedient service, it is a testament of our commitment to and our passion for living out the will of God.

According to Matthew 28:19-20, we have an important job to do for God, but many of us have not responded to the call. "Go ye therefore, and teach all nations, baptizing them in the name of the Father, and of the Son, and of the Holy Ghost: Teaching them to observe all things whatsoever I have commanded you:

and, lo, I am with you alway, even unto the end of the world. Amen." When it comes to God's command and God's instructions we must respond like Isaiah, Mary, and Jesus.

In the sixth chapter of the book of Isaiah, God poses a question in the eighth verse that we'd be wise to read and then structure our responses in the same manner as Isaiah's response. "Also I heard the voice of the Lord, saying, Whom shall I send, and who will go for us? Then said I, Here am I; send me." Isaiah's response was one of service derived from gratitude. Our response to God should be the same. "Send me, Lord, I'll go for you. I love and appreciate all that you've done for me. I want you to know that you can count on me. Send me!"

In the first chapter of Luke the story of Mary learning that she'd be the mother of Jesus is beautifully recorded. She is greeted by the angel of the Lord and given news that is beyond hard to believe or comprehend. She doesn't understand everything nor is everything explained to her either, but her response is powerful! "And Mary said, 'Behold the handmaid of the Lord; be it unto me according to thy word'. And the angel departed from her." (Luke 1:38) Her response to this bombshell of news that has been dropped into her lap is, "Okay, whatever the Lord wants me to do I'm willing to do it." That type of response allows God to bless us in ways we never thought possible. I'm sure Mary didn't comprehend what it would mean to be the mother of our Lord. I'm sure she didn't know how everything would play out, but her response is one of faith and dependence. God desires that we have the same type of response when He comes to us with our mission's instructions.

It was the worse night ever. Jesus knew what was about to happen in only a few hours. He knew that it wouldn't be much longer before guards would come and seize him. He knew that they would beat him within an inch of his life. He knew that the thorns from the crown that they'd make to mock him would be placed on his head and pierce his temple. He knew about the insults he'd hear from the crowd, and worse, the hurt he'd feel from being abandoned by those who said that they loved him, in the toughest moment of his life. He prayed and prayed. He watched the men that he'd spent the past few years mentoring struggle to show enough commitment to stay awake and pray with him. His thoughts were everywhere, yet he knew that he had to remain focused on the mission at hand. So what was his response to his forthcoming torture and eventual death? His words still give me chills. In the face of death he presses on and he utters words that should inspire us all. "Saying, 'Father, if thou be willing, remove this cup from me: nevertheless not my will, but thine, be done'" (Luke 22:42). Our response must be like Jesus' response. It's not about us; it is about God. I will respond by obeying the Lord even unto death. Thank you, Jesus, for responding with obedience, for it was your obedience that saved my soul.

God responded to our need of deliverance by sending His son to die a horrible death so that we could be released from our sins. Now it is time that we respond. We must respond with an emphatic "YES". We must respond like Isaiah, and let God know that we are accountable. We must let God know that if He needs a soldier we're ready to carry out the mission. We must respond like Mary. We might not have all of the details, but when Jesus is leading we don't need all of the details. He's proven himself to be trustworthy and so we must respond with a decisive "YES." We must respond with the understanding that what God desires in our lives is the best thing for our lives. We must respond like Jesus. The road will get weary at times. But Jesus never faltered, and He never failed. He remained focused on His mission, He remained faithful to God, and He remained fired up for the things of the kingdom of God. Because of His response, we now have the ability to respond likewise. Today is the day that we must respond to God out of a grateful heart, because tomorrow is not promised.

REFLECT AND CONNECT

1. What other characters in the Bible can you think of who responded in ways that has had an impact on your faith?
2. What is the worst response that we can give God after learning of what He's done for us? What is the best response?
3. Because of Jesus' response, we all can be saved. What will be your response to His saving sacrifice?

CONNECT WITH THE AUTHOR

Email me your questions or concerns about this chapter or share with me how this chapter blessed you.
got2liveright@gmail.com

Tell the world your thoughts about this chapter. Don't forget to mention me @ccody3 so I can connect with you.

CHAPTER 12

RETURN

return: to bring, give, send, or take (something) to the place that it came from or the place where it should go
Merriam-Webster Dictionary

Years ago Michael Jordan retired from the Chicago Bulls and the fate of the NBA seemed uncertain. Jordan was the face of the league. He was an icon. When he departed to chase his dream of playing baseball, the league still remained but it wasn't the same. Then rumors that Jordan was going to return to the league began to surface, and once they did, fans became restless with enthusiasm at the good news. When Air Jordan stepped back on the court, it was like everything was right in the basketball universe again. The moon and sun seemed to shine brighter than before; the birds seemed to chirp more loudly and with melodies that had been reserved for such an occasion. As wonderful as Jordan's return was to the NBA, it doesn't come close to comparing to how glorious it will be when Jesus returns for those who love and accept Him.

The greatest hope of every believer is that one day Jesus will return to balance the books, to impart justice in all the areas that had seemed to evaporate, and to make everything right, and ultimately to take them to Heaven with Him. Many men and women have sacrificed their lives willingly with no fear and with unbelievable joy because they longed for the return of our Lord and Savior Jesus Christ. Because we also believe so strongly that He will return, we strive to live lives that are pleasing to Him. We strive to live above reproach. We press forward when the world tells us to give up and quit. Because we know with certainty (faith) that He will return, we gain the strength to endure the hardships that we may face in our lives.

In John's Gospel, John records a powerful statement that Jesus made to his disciples that has been a source of excitement and encouragement for every disciple since. "And if I go and prepare a place for you, I will come again, and receive you unto myself; that where I am, *there* ye may be also" (John 14:3). In this passage, Jesus is once again trying to explain to His disciples that He is going to have to leave them but only temporarily. He makes it crystal clear that He will return. Jesus ensures them just as he desires to ensure us that he will return for us so that we can be where He is.

The funny thing is that people will wrack their brains trying to pinpoint exactly when they should expect this return. Instead of living holy lives that will ensure that we are prepared for His return no matter when that day may be, we'd rather expend all of our energy and power trying to search for information that is unattainable according to Matthew 24:36, "But of that day and hour knoweth no *man*, no, not the angels of Heaven, but my Father only."

There have been many men in the past who have led people astray with their predictions about the return of Christ or when the world would come to an end. I remember how the prediction of Y2K had so many in an uproar. I wonder how many of them still have cans of Spam tucked away in the cellar or basement. If only we'd learn to believe God instead of man. If only we'd come to trust that God has never failed us and that He always keeps His word. "God *is* not a man, that He should lie; neither the son of man, that He should repent: hath He said, and shall He not do *it*? or hath He spoken, and shall He not make it good?" (Numbers 23:19) I believe with all of my heart that Jesus will return. This belief enables me to honor God when it doesn't connect to logic. Something I've had to learn is that faith supersedes logic. Oftentimes, what God instructs and requires doesn't make sense to the world or to worldly people. But because I trust Him so much and since He told me that He would return, I have made up my mind to honor Him with my lifestyle regardless of the circumstances of my life.

The Bible is full of stories of major returns and the impact of those returns. Another of my favorite parables or stories in the Bible is the story of the prodigal son. In this story a man has two sons whom he loves very much. The younger son decides to request his inheritance from his father early. It appears that he had come to a point where he no longer wants to live under his father's rule. The father gives the son what he asks for and the young man set out to live his life to the fullest. He finds himself surrounded with many friends. These friends are very good at helping him spend up his money. He could hang out at all the cool spots, and hit up all the clubs. He bought drinks for everyone! He has a "Don't look on the value menu, whatever you want just order it!" attitude. The Bible explains that he spent all he had on riotous living. Here's another nugget of wisdom to grab ahold to and never let go of. ANYTIME YOU GET AWAY FROM THE PROTECTION OF THE FATHER'S HOUSE, DEVASTATION AND POSSIBLY DESTRUCTION ARE SURE TO COME.

This young man finds himself feeding the pigs to earn a few bucks in order to survive. This was a big NO-NO for his culture. Young men of his cultural background never dealt with pigs. The story gets even more gloomy! The young man is starving and starts to contemplate eating the slop that he was about to throw out for the pigs to eat. The first 6 words of Luke 15:17 are maybe the most impactful six words that one can read when it comes to getting right in life. "And when he came to himself..." Here is a young man who had a good life when he was connected to his father. He didn't want for anything. He couldn't think of a time that he experienced lack. But now he finds himself in the lowest state that he's ever been in. As he puts the pigs' food to his mouth to end his hunger pains, his noses catches a whiff of the foul odor of the pigs' favorite dish and his mind immediately flashed back to his father's home. He begins to remember what things used to be like and how he wishes he could have that again.

Oftentimes, our return to God is held off until we get a whiff of the foul odor that sin has left in our lives. Our surroundings may be different, but our solution will be always be the same. Maybe you're not in a pig pen; maybe you're living in the penthouse of a luxurious hotel when the stench of sin overwhelms you. Whether you reside in the pig pen or the penthouse, the way out of this for both persons is wrapped up in those six words found in Luke 15:17. We must come to ourselves. And when we do, our next move will become obvious. WE MUST RETURN TO OUR FATHER'S HOUSE.

When Michael Jordan returned to the Chicago Bulls after retiring and trying his hand at baseball, the NBA experienced an immediate revival. Excitement and enthusiasm about the game gripped the fans once more. The King of the Court was coming back; he was returning and the league desperately needed him. The same way the fans were overjoyed at the return of MJ, believers find ourselves full of anticipation as we await the return of Jesus. We are overjoyed because we know that when Jesus returns, everything will once again be made right.

There are several parables or stories that Jesus told about His return. He wanted to break things down on a level that those that were listening could understand and also apply. He wanted them to know (and He wants us to know, as well) that His return is certain and our eternal destination needs to be certain, too. There is no need to hope and wonder if you will be one of the ones He returns for. He laid out the blueprint for living the type of life that will ensure your place in the kingdom.

Parable after parable and story after story were spoken so we'd grasp the urgency of getting ready and staying ready for His return.

In Matthew 25:1-13, Jesus tells a parable about ten virgins who were waiting for the bridegroom to come. Five of them secured oil for their lamps (they were prepared) and the other five did not secure oil for their lamps (they were unprepared). All ten had the same opportunity to be ready when the bridegroom came, but only half seized the opportunity. It appears that our generations are experiencing the same issues. Many are choosing to remain unprepared when the announcement has been made that the bridegroom (Jesus) will soon be coming. He will soon return for His bride (The Church). When the alarm was sounded that the bridegroom was coming, five were filled with hope and anticipation while the other five were filled with panic and dread. The bible calls the five who were prepared wise and the five that remained unprepared fools. Matthew 25:13 has always been a passage of scripture that motivated me to be ready and stay ready for our Lord's return. "Watch therefore, for ye know neither the day nor the hour wherein the Son of man cometh."

You don't have to look far to find another powerful illustration about the return of Jesus. In fact, just start reading the next few verses. In Matthew 25:14-34, Jesus tells another jaw-dropping story. He explains how a traveler is about to go on a long trip, so he calls in his servants and gives them each talents. To one servant he gives five, another two, and to the last servant the traveler gives one talent. After some time, the traveler returns and he wants to see what each servant has done with the talents that were left. The first servant with five talents takes what his master left him and gets busy and produces five more talents. The second servant with two talents also works with what he has and he confidently brings his master two more talents. As the third servant slowly approaches his master, the master smiles in anticipation of what this man has to show, but then his smile quickly turns into a frown. The servant quickly tries to explain why he hadn't done anything before the master returned. Whatever you do, DO NOT MISS THIS NEXT POINT. When the master returns, it is too late for explanation; what He expects is preparation. We must be prepared for the return of our Lord and Savior Jesus Christ. We don't know when that time will come. And truthfully, that isn't what we should exert our energies on trying to calculate. Rather, we should muster all of our strength and desire for reading and studying the words of God found in the pages of the Holy Bible to instruct us on how to live holy and upright lives so that no matter when He returns, we will be ready.

REFLECT AND CONNECT

1. How does knowing that Jesus will return motivate you to live for God?
2. Read Matthew 25:14-34. Do you identify more with the servants who used their talents to be productive or the one who hid his talent?
3. What will you do differently to ensure you are ready for Jesus' return?

CONNECT WITH THE AUTHOR

Email me your questions or concerns about this chapter or share with me how this chapter blessed you.
got2liveright@gmail.com

Tell the world your thoughts about this chapter. Don't forget to mention me @ccody3 so I can connect with you.

CHAPTER 13

REVEAL

reveal: to show (something) plainly or clearly; to make (something that was hidden) able to be seen
Merriam-Webster Dictionary

When Jesus returns, not only will everything be made right, but He will make known to us the things that have been a mystery while we walked the earth. To be honest, I believe that we will be so overjoyed about being with Him that we won't really care to seek the answers to the questions that overwhelm us right now. Everyone has questions. Everyone wants answers. And in the end, God will reveal to us what things meant in our lives and why things happened the way they did in our lives. In 1 Corinthians 13:12, Paul explains how we see but we don't see all. "For now we see through a glass, darkly; but then face to face: now I know in part; but then shall I know even as also I am known." In the end, we will understand. In the end, things will be made clear to us. No longer will we see only a glimpse of what God has to show; we will see it all.

One thing that I've learned as I've walked with God is that He knows best! He knows how much of our journey we can bear to see. He knows that if He were to reveal everything to us all at once that we would mess things up. And because He knows all things, he knows the exact time to reveal the exact things we need to experience in our lives. It's sort of like this: As parents, we love the excitement on our children's faces as the Christmas holidays approach and our youngsters are filled with awe and amazement about Santa. At two or three years old, they believe without hesitation that there is a man who wears a red suit, who rides in a sleigh pulled by reindeer; his main job is to deliver bags of toys to the good boys and girls once a year. But there will come a time when our children will be ready to handle the news: MAMA and DADDY are Santa! We worked overtime for you to have the G.I. Joe with the Kung Fu grip!

If only our children would take that same awe and amazement that they had toward Santa and redirect it toward their parents. Once our beautiful bundles of joy receive the revelation of what Mama and Daddy have gone through to give them those special gifts, you'd think they'd honor us with all the strength they could muster. Don't lose heart, my fellow parents. Sometimes it takes time for the revelation to sink in.

It's funny because God has continued to give us revelations and they have yet to sink in to a point that we offer Him the honor that He is due. I truly believe that until we really get a revelation what Jesus did for us (I like to say "me" to make it personal) on the cross, we will never show Him the reverence that He deserves. We utter the words so casually that "Jesus died to save me from my sins." But we continue to walk in those sins

94

with no intentions of repentance or turning away from them and turning back to God and His ways.

One of my favorite incidents in which Jesus revealed Himself is in Acts 9. While Saul was on his way to Damascus to hunt down and take down anyone who claimed to be a Christian, Jesus revealed himself in a powerful and life changing way. I like to say that all of us need to have a "Damascus Road experience". All of this time Saul thought he knew God and what God wanted for his life. He thought that he was living a good enough life. One of the greatest tricks or ploys of the enemy is to convince us that we are living "good enough". But when God reveals Himself to us, it will shine a light on our sin and how short we fall of the mark. If we are honest with ourselves, we will respond with humility and shame. Revelation that is accepted always leads to repentance and repentance always leads to change. In Acts 9, we see that Saul was knocked down from his animal and was blinded by a great light. He heard a voice that asked him why he was hunting down and harming the Christian people. Before this revelation took place, Saul thought that what he was doing was his greatest service to God. After this revelation took place, he'd find out and carry out his greatest service to God. The man who killed men and women who claimed the name of Jesus Christ would go on to write the majority of the books in the New Testament. Wow! Here's a revelation for you: What could God do in your life if you'd allow Him to? Before God could use Saul, He had to knock him down from his high horse (pun intended) and change the way he saw things. He had sight but yet he was blind; now God chose to blind him so that He could give him a new vision! There aren't too many men in the Bible who possessed the type of zeal to complete their mission for God like Saul gained after God revealed to him who Jesus was and what his mission would be. Revelation leads to repentance and repentance leads to change. Three things changed for Saul after this revealing of the Christ: his name, his mindset, and his mission.

After this Damascus road experience he would no longer be called Saul but now he'd go by the name Paul. Sometimes we need to be called something different to take advantage of our fresh new start in life. In one of my 2nd grade classes many years ago, I had a student who was very mischievous. His first, middle, and last name could have easily been "Get In Trouble." He could be found in or near the principal's office daily. They tried everything to help get this young man's behavior on track. I'll never forget the day that he came to my class and began to make some poor behavior choices when I called out his name. He immediately stopped me and said that he no longer went by that name and that all of the teachers were now calling him by his new name. He informed me that the plan was put in place so that he could have a fresh start. I remember laughing inside and thinking that it wouldn't take long before his behavior tarnished his new name. We can change our names every day for the rest of our lives, but nothing about us will change until we change our mindset and our mission in life as well.

In Philippians 2:5, Paul writes "Let this mind be in you, which was also in Christ Jesus." He started out as a man who wanted to do nothing but destroy anyone who was connected to Christ, but he finished his life as a man who wanted nothing more than to build up all mankind so that they'd come to know Christ. It's amazing what can happen in a man's life once Christ reveals Himself to that man. His mindset allowed him to accept and carry out his new mission. The mission was simple: seek out those who don't know God and lead them to God through Jesus Christ. The gospel that he was so zealous about stopping had become his greatest joy to impart. When God reveals himself to us as He did with Paul, our lives will no longer be the same IF we will allow God to change our names, our mindsets, and our missions.

Revelation doesn't come to everyone the same way. Sometimes God reveals things to us as we listen to the minister preach during worship. Sometimes God shows us His hand at work during our quiet time with Him on our lunch break. The important thing is that whenever and wherever God chooses to reveal something to us, we must be open to Him and ready and willing to obey. It could be that our unwillingness to obey is keeping God from revealing to us His desires for our lives. There is no need for God to show us the steps to take when we are fixed on standing still.

Another great revelation that God longs to show us concerns the spiritual gifts that He has placed within us. Have you ever looked at the life of other believers who were using the gifts that God placed in their lives and wished you knew what God had in store for you? You may have even prayed a time or two and asked God to show you the gifts and talents that He has given you. I believe that one of the things that God wants to do for His people more than anything is to reveal to them the gifts that He's entrusted them with and what He desires for them to do with those gifts. I also believe that we keep God from being able to fulfill this in our lives because we don't have a willingness to obey and live for Him. And so all of that wonderful potential remains locked within us and it remains untapped until God is able to reveal this to us. We've got to ask the same two questions of God that Saul asked in Acts 22:8, 10, "Who art thou Lord... and What shall I do, Lord?" If we sincerely ask God these questions, He will answer us. He will reveal to us who He is and He will reveal to us what He wants us to do. After God gives us this revelation it is then up to us to honor Him and obey Him.

Before Jesus humbly rode into Jerusalem to allow his life to be sacrificed for the sins of all mankind, he shared a very intimate moment with his disciples. He asked them "Whom do men say that I am?" (Mark 8:27) He was about to open their eyes to another important truth – one that, once truly understood, would give these men the strength and courage to follow God even unto the point of death. We cannot serve God through the revelation that He's given to another. If we allow Him to, He will reveal Himself to us personally. "And he saith unto them, 'But whom say ye that I am?' And Peter answereth and saith unto him, 'Thou art the Christ.'" (Mark 8:29)

The way we *see* Jesus will determine the way we *serve* Jesus. Peter knew the right thing to say, but Peter didn't really understand what he was saying. Jesus explained to Peter that he got the answer correct. "And Jesus answered and said unto him, 'Blessed art thou, Simon Bar-jonah: for flesh and blood hath not revealed it unto thee, but my Father which is in heaven.'" (Matthew 16:17) But how many of us realize that having the right answers doesn't mean we're going to make the right decisions?

Jesus longs to reveal who He really is to us as well. Just think, He walked side by side with the 12 men He hand-picked for 3 years and they still didn't completely get who He was. He had shown them things that would blow our minds: fish overflowing the boat, wind obeying his voice, demons leaping into pigs, water turned into the best wine ever tasted, even the dead man Lazarus rising out of the grave to live again, and they STILL DIDN'T UNDERSTAND WHO HE WAS! Once Jesus was crucified and after He resurrected from the tomb and revealed Himself to the disciples again, it began to sink in. The understanding of who they walked with and talked with all those years was starting to make sense. Jesus told them that He was the Son of God, He had shown them that He was the Son of God, and now they understood that He was the Son of God. When that light bulb of revelation takes place, your life will change forever. No longer will you feel comfortable in your sin. No longer will you live as though anything goes. When you really understand the revelation of who Jesus is and how much

He loves you, you will desire to completely and totally live for Him.

My pastor once preached a message that sent my imagination into overdrive and sent chills down my spine. He was speaking of Revelation 4:8, in which the angels in Heaven never ceased from saying "Holy, Holy, Holy." He painted the most beautiful and powerful picture of the angels bowing before the throne of God, and when they came up God revealed something new to them, something about Him they'd never seen before – something wonderful, something beautiful – and this made them bow again and again and again in honor. It is amazing how fast we become bored with God's majesty or how quickly we become so familiar with God that His power and might doesn't inspire our worship. Could it be that we've never truly received a revelation of who God is? That message from years ago has stuck with me. I pray that I never become desensitized to how awesome God is. One of the coolest things about studying God's Word, which reminds me of the angel illustration that my pastor demonstrated in his sermon, is that we can read the same passage of scripture over and over, yet each time God can reveal to us something new and exciting concerning that passage.

I was reading a book in the past titled *90 Minutes in Heaven* by Don Piper and it blew my mind. In this book, the author who is also a preacher, explains how he'd died and gone to Heaven for 90 minutes. The things that God had revealed to him made him sad and depressed that God would allow him to return to earth. After taking a tour of Heaven and seeing what things in the Kingdom were like, he didn't want to come back here. Who could blame him? But according to another revelation that God gave him, his return was ordered so that he could tell his story. I have no doubt that his testimony and his book will lead to many others entering into the kingdom of God one day. I remember having a conversation once with my father (who is also a Baptist preacher) and he told me of a book titled *23 Minutes in Hell* by Bill Wiese. I haven't had the opportunity to read this one yet, but his description of the book was captivating. Just as God gave Mr. Piper a tour of Heaven, He gave Mr. Wiese a tour of Hell. He revealed to this man what Hell is like so that he could encourage those that would listen to avoid this place at all cost! Long before Bill Wiese had his experience, God gave John (one of Jesus' disciples) a revelation of what the end times would be like. It just so happens to be the last book of the Bible and it is even titled Revelation.

Many people will either love Revelation (some to a point of obsession) or avoid the words that John penned because they fear the content. I admit that Revelation can be quite confusing and requires indepth studying. I must also confess I have not spent a lot of time trying to understand what all of the symbolism in Revelation means, but I do try to live an upright, holy and obedient lifestyle so that no matter when Jesus returns and all of the symbolism that was revealed to John is fulfilled, I AM READY. The Bible is filled with undeniable warnings and also great promises; it is God's desire to reveal these warnings and promises to us, but in order for that to happen we're going to have to commit to spending time in the Word of God. Think about it: If you knew you had treasure in your backyard, would you ever stop digging for it? Well, there is a great treasure to be found within the pages of the Bible. Are you willing to dig?

REFLECT AND CONNECT

1. What is the greatest thing God has revealed to you about your life?
2. Have you ever asked God to reveal to you His special mission for your life? If not, take a moment and seek God in prayer and ask Him for your orders. Make this your daily prayer. "Father: what will you have me to do today?"
3. Have you ever taken the time to ask God to reveal to you the special gifts that He has placed within you? We cannot give God the service that He deserves if we don't utilize the gifts that He's given us to honor Him. Ask Him to show you what your gifting is and ask Him to help you use your gifts wisely and properly for the kingdom's purposes.

CONNECT WITH THE AUTHOR

Email me your questions or concerns about this chapter or share with me how this chapter blessed you. got2liveright@gmail.com

Tell the world your thoughts about this chapter. Don't forget to mention me @ccody3 so I can connect with you.

CHAPTER 14

REWARD

reward: something that is given in return for good
or evil done or received or that is offered or given for
some service or attainment
Merriam-Webster Dictionary

Why do we do the things that we do? Most people desire to be recognized and rewarded for their efforts. And if a reward isn't attached to the outcome of an event, it is unfortunate that many of us will not see value participating. As a school teacher I find myself in the midst of many teachable moments. One day one of my students was showing me a beautiful ring that he had recently acquired. He explained to me that his mother worked for a storage facility and that when people didn't pay for their storage, they'd remove the people's items from the storage units. It just so happened that his mom got him this ring through a situation where someone never returned to get their items from storage. As I looked at the ring I could see that it was a bowling State Championship ring from a local private school. After examining the ring for a quick minute, I noticed that the year of the championship and the initials of the athlete who won this prestigious award were engraved on the side of the ring. I asked my student if he ever thought about finding the person to whom the ring belonged and returning it, but he gave me a look that showed he had no interest in giving it back. I asked him that if I could find the rightful owner would he be willing to return the ring. His response was quick and certain, "Only if he gives me a reward."

It took me only five minutes to find out who the ring belonged to and how to reach the person. I searched the archives of the school for their recent bowling teams. I matched up the year on the ring to the year on the screen. I scanned through the roster and there it was: the initials on the ring matched those of one of the bowlers on the team. I then searched Facebook and found the person's name. He was now a college student in Knoxville, Tennessee. I skimmed through the bio on Facebook to be sure it was the same person. I saw that he was a former student at the same local private school and at that point I was sure that I'd found the owner of the ring. The young man in my class was playing soccer with his peers when I called him over to explain the results of my superb detective skills. I explained how I'd located the rightful owner of the ring and asked if I had his permission to reach out to the other young man. He was uneasy about giving it back, but he agreed it would be okay to try to make contact only if he got a reward. "Isn't doing the right thing enough reward?" I asked. He looked at me with eyes that were stunned and confused – like the question I had asked was in a foreign language. That look made it painfully clear to me that doing the right thing without expecting a reward in return is a foreign concept for so many of us.

This encounter with my student reminded me of a time when Jesus was teaching about doing good deeds and attempting to get God's attention. He explained that we shouldn't do good in front of others for a pat on the back. "Watch out! Don't do your good deeds publicly, to be admired by others, for you will lose the reward from your Father in heaven." (Matthew 6:1 NLT) Our motives are oftentimes more important to God than our actions. Who cares if you do this good thing for someone if your motive behind it is "not so good"? When Jesus died on the cross for the sins of the world, he did it knowing that everyone was NOT going to give their lives in return. He didn't die only for those who would live for Him. He loved the world and so He died to save every man who would believe in and live for Him. His motives were pure.

God is not against rewards. He loves to reward His people. In Hebrews 11:6, Paul explains how we can be rewarded by God: "But without faith it is impossible to please Him: for he that cometh to God must believe that He is, and that He is a rewarder of them that diligently seek Him." Just as I told my student that doing the right thing is a reward in itself, seeking after God and pursuing a godly life opens the door for a life filled with rewards! The key word in Hebrews 11:6 is diligently. There is something special about watching a sports movie in which the person who perseveres or the team that remains diligent in its training wins in the end. It stirs the very souls of men. Everyone loves the *Rocky* movies because we observe a man fight for what he believes in. And with all the odds stacked against him, he never falters or gives up. He remains diligent and he is rewarded with victory!

Our reward is dependent upon our resolve. It's not how one starts a race that is noteworthy; it is how one finishes that race that matters. You don't earn a reward because you stood on the starting blocks. The reward is given to those who finish the race. The old story "The Tortiose and the Hare" paints a beautiful picture of diligence being rewarded. Slow and steady wins the race. If we stay focused and stay on the path before us and, if we don't give up, we will also be rewarded. "So let's not get tired of doing what is good. At just the right time we will reap a harvest of blessing if we don't give up." (Galatians 6:9 NLT) It may appear that everything around you is falling apart and it may look like you aren't getting ahead in life. But when you do an intense self-assessment, you can truthfully say that spiritually you're doing the things that you're supposed to do. You pay your tithe at your church, you haven't missed a Sunday in 10 years, you serve as an usher and a Sunday School teacher, but it seems like nothing is going right for you. It is in moments like these that you will be persuaded by the enemy to throw in the towel and just do what feels right to you even if it's wrong according to God. Again in the book of Hebrews, Paul writes to encourage the people that they can't go wrong if they trust in God. "So do not throw away your confidence; it will be richly rewarded." (Hebrews 10:35 NIV) The reward will surely come, if we can outlast the temptation to quit.

Something that we would be wise to remember is that sacrifice is always rewarded. Let's examine how the sacrifice that Jesus made was rewarded. The Bible explains that because of His sacrifice, Jesus now sits at the right hand of God and now the name of Jesus is above every name! "That at the name of Jesus every knee should bow, of things in Heaven, and things in earth, and things under the earth; And that every tongue should confess that Jesus Christ is Lord, to the glory of God the Father." (Philippians 2:10-11) His sacrifice was worth the reward. Our sacrifices are worth the reward! "For I reckon that the sufferings of this present time are not worthy to be compared with the glory which shall be revealed in us." (Romans 8:18) If we will commit to diligently seek after God, He promises that He will make it worth our while. He promises that the reward that He has for us will far outweigh any trouble that we face in this world.

Knowing that I will be rewarded for my efforts, my struggles, my pains, and even my triumphs empowers me to continue searching after God and His ways with my whole heart. I strive to live a life that shows how grateful I am to God for what He has done for me through Christ Jesus. I recognize that everything in my life is not going to work out perfectly, but everything in my life will work out. "And we know that God causes everything to work together for the good of those who love God and are called according to His purpose for them." (Romans 8:28 NLT) Knowing that one day everything I've endured will be examined, assessed and rewarded gives me the courage and faith to hang on, hold on, and press on. The reward and benefit of following and serving God have convinced me that living for Him each day that He allows me to open my eyes is the only possible response I can offer.

"Well done", are two words that I desire to hear the Lord say to me when my time on this earth has come to an end. "His lord said unto him, Well done, good and faithful servant; thou hast been faithful over a few things, I will make thee ruler over many things: enter thou into the joy of thy lord." (Matthew 25:23) In this verse the word *faithful* is used in a similar way that the word *diligently* was used in the previous verse. Our reward will not be awarded if we do not remain faithful. Faithfulness is one of the chief characteristics of God and lack of faithfulness is one of the chief character flaws found in man. God remains faithful to us even though we've failed Him. God grants mercy and grace to all men, but the rewards of God are reserved for the faithful.

If you could imagine a reward that you thought would totally satisfy your every whim, you still wouldn't scratch the surface of how God can reward you for your diligent and consistent service. "But as it is written, 'Eye hath not seen, nor ear heard, neither have entered into the heart of man, the things which God hath prepared for them that love him.'" (1 Corinthians 2:9 KJV) God is the great rewarder. His rewards will exceed our expectations. You can search through the scriptures and you'll find numerous stories about when God's blessing exceeded the people's requests. The Children of Israel's wilderness experience and Naaman's battle with leprosy are two of many powerful lessons.

The Children of Israel had been slaves in Egypt for many years. And then they cried out to God. Crying out to God always gets God's attention, but getting right with God is what gets God's reward. They wanted to be rescued and wanted out from under the oppressive hands of Pharaoh and the Egyptian rule. And so what does God do? He shows up and He shows out! He sends many plagues upon the Egyptian kingdom until Pharaoh finally relents and frees God's chosen people. They march out of Egypt with a freedom that they didn't earn but only asked for. Not long after being free they find themselves in a bind. The sea is in front of them so they can't go forward. The mountains are at the right and left, and when they turn to look back, Pharaoh's army is quickly approaching to destroy them. The people begin to complain and cry out. How quickly they forgot how God had just freed them from the harsh hands of Pharaoh.

Before we judge them, we must think about our own lives. Do we find ourselves looking back and complaining because we don't know what God has coming up next in our lives? So what does God do next? Brace yourself for this one! He sends a wind to blow over the waters. The water stands up straight and forms two walls, providing a path for the people to walk through. One of my favorite parts of this story is how the Bible explains that the people walked across on dry ground. God was so good to them that he didn't even make them walk in the mud! After all of God's people made it across to the other side, Pharaoh's chariots were allowed to continue to follow them. When every chariot had entered the path in the sea that God provided for Israel, God released the waters. The Bible tells us that all of Pharaoh's men were drowned. Israel was safe, their enemy was defeated, and God was honored (for the moment at least). Now safe on the other side of the sea, the Children of Israel find themselves getting hungry, so God provides Manna (a delightful bread made fresh daily and delivered from Heaven). After eating this for a couple days, they complain about the bread so God provides birds for meat. I mean the birds literally came to the people to give up their lives so that they could have a two piece snack and a biscuit. When was the last time your dinner came to you? God had been so good to these people and God has been so good to us, as well. We treat God the same way that the Children of Israel did. We take the reward of God and then we forget about revering to the rewarder.

The story of Naaman can be found in the fifth chapter of 2 Kings. I've always loved this story and the many lessons that can learned from it. Naaman was a captain in the king of Aram's army. He had a horrible and incurable skin disease called leprosy. In those days getting diagnosed with leprosy was a death sentence. A young Israelite girl who had been taken captive worked in his home. She went to Naaman's wife and recommended that he go to speak with the prophet in Israel. She explains how the prophet could heal Naaman. What's the worst that can happen, right? He takes this news to his king, and because the king honors and respects Naaman, he writes a letter to the king of Israel to request that the king allow Naaman to come and be healed of this terrible disease.

Fast forward a few verses to find Naaman approaching the prophet's home. The prophet sends out a messenger to give Naaman specific instructions to follow to regain his health. Naaman is taken aback somewhat, because he assumed the prophet would come out personally and speak to him. After all, he is an important man back where he came from. The instructions were relayed but they were weird. He is instructed to go to the Jordan River and dip himself in the water seven times to be healed. Again Naaman finds himself irritated. He voices his displeasure by stating that there were pools of water back home that are much better than the dirty waters of the Jordan. What was wrong with the water back home? He leaves with no desire to carry out the instructions when his men plead with him to give it a try. It's not like the prophet told him to do something difficult. All he had to do was dip in the water seven times. The Bible doesn't say this, but in my imagination I could see Naaman wade out into the river until the warm dirty water reaches his waistline. "Here goes nothing," he mumbles and then he starts dipping his head into the water, but with each dip, he thinks to himself how foolish he must look. One dip, then two, three, and so on but when he comes up after the seventh dip, something feels different. He feels different. He doesn't have a mirror but he can't wait to get out of the water to see what has happened. As he pushes through the water, heading back to shore, he can see the look in the eyes of his men. Some of the men are in tears while others have smiles from ear to ear. "Did it work? What are you smiling about? Give me the mirror;

let me see!" As I stated earlier, God's rewards will exceed our expectations. "So he went down and dipped himself in the Jordan seven times, as the man of God had told him, and his flesh was restored and became clean like that of a young boy." (2 Kings 5:14 NIV) Not only did God reward him with healing, his skin was renewed. His skin was revitalized. He looked like a young man again. God knows how to reward!

The greatest reward that God wants to grant is eternal life. He sent Jesus to die the most horrific death to ensure that all men that call on His name can receive this reward. "And it shall come to pass, that whosoever shall call on the name of the Lord shall be saved." (Acts 2:21 KJV) After He died and resurrected from the grave, Jesus told his disciples that he had to leave them but it was only to go and prepare a place for them. "And if I go and prepare a place for you, I will come back and take you to be with me that you also may be where I am." (John 14:3 NIV) The reward of eternal life and eternal communion and fellowship with God is a reward worth living and dying for. Every one of the men Jesus selected to follow him endured and suffered hardship and even horrible deaths because of their connection to Christ. Every one of them remained faithful to God after they truly understood the revelation of who Christ was. And now every one of them has received his reward for faithfulness to God.

You can be rewarded with eternal life today, as well. It's a reward that has been purchased for you and set aside until you decide to ask for it. However, such a great reward does require a great commitment. Jesus gave up his life so that we can be rewarded eternal life with Him and the Father. "For Christ also suffered once for sins, the righteous for the unrighteous, to bring you to God. He was put to death in the body but made alive in the Spirit." (1 Peter 3:18 NIV) He (The Righteous One) traded places with us (The Unrighteous Ones) so that we can have a place with him, but we have to ask for it. And when he gives it to us, we must live for him. And when it's all said and done, we will receive the reward of eternal life in the kingdom of Heaven like those who have gone on before us.

REFLECT AND CONNECT

1. What will it take for you to go from serving God *for the reward* to serving God "just because you love Him"?
2. When you do good deeds, what are the real motives behind your actions? Would you continue doing these things if you weren't recognized for what you did?
3. Are there any rewards that the world can offer (money, fame, prestige, etc.) worth forfeiting rewards that God offers (peace, power, eternal life, etc.)?

CONNECT WITH THE AUTHOR

Email me your questions or concerns about this chapter or share with me how this chapter blessed you.
got2liveright@gmail.com

Tell the world your thoughts about this chapter. Don't forget to mention me @ecody3 so I can connect with you.

CONCLUSION

The Bible is a book of salvation. Although none of the principles that were reviewed in this book were given the title of salvation, they all lead to salvation or are given to those who are saved.

We have all sinned and **REBELLED** against God; because of this, we all need to be redeemed.

Nothing that we can do will earn us **REDEMPTION**. Our redemption was settled when Jesus gave up his life as the ultimate sacrifice for sin.

Once we realize the price that has been paid for us, it should lead us to **REPENT**. Conviction won't cut it, confession won't cut it, and contrition won't cut it! We must repent and turn away from our sins and turn back to God. Repentance should come easily to us when we acknowledge that we didn't deserve to be redeemed, but we were included anyway.

Once we repent, we are **REBORN**! Hallelujah! We are new men and new women. We get a fresh start. Everything we did or everything that we used to be means nothing any longer.

Once we are reborn and adopted into the household of faith, God can **RESTORE** us to the position that He intended for us. There's no greater feeling than the warm embrace of restoration. Do you feel overwhelmed with gratitude yet?

Well, go ahead and **REJOICE**! Shout out loud, "Thank you, Jesus!" Go ahead – bow before Him and tell Him how great his is. He deserves it.

Don't forget that God is going to have to **REPLACE** some things that are trying to stick around in your life. You're going to have to allow Him to take away some things that are slowing you down and install the things that will increase your ability to live for Him.

The best way to stay on track is to **REMEMBER** what God has done and remind yourself of the things that He wants to do in your life.

Don't be surprised when the devil starts attacking you; just **RESIST** him. He'll leave – the Bible promises us that. Don't argue with him; just resist him and watch him scamper on his way. But stay on guard because he's going to come again with something else up his sleeve.

But if you **REMAIN** in God and walk in the Spirit, you'll be ready for that attack as well. So what's your answer?

How will you **RESPOND** to God's call on your life now that He's redeemed you, restored you, and replaced the garbage in your life with abundant blessings? Will you follow Him with your whole heart or will you come up with another reason to do what seems right in your eyes?

Don't forget that Jesus will **RETURN** for all of those who have returned to him and those who have responded to His call.

His return will be glorious! In fact, at that time, everything will be **REVEALED** to us. All questions will be answered and all wrongs will be made right.

All sins will be brought up and dealt with and all of those that have remained righteous will receive their **REWARD**. Now, who said the Bible is hard to understand?

Made in the USA
Lexington, KY
30 June 2016